For our friend

ELIZABETH LAWRENCE KALASHNIKOFF

with our love

ALL THE HAPPY ENDINGS

Books by Helen and George Papashvily

ANYTHING CAN HAPPEN

YES AND NO STORIES

THANKS TO NOAH

DOGS AND PEOPLE

ALL THE HAPPY ENDINGS

A study of the domestic novel in America, the women who wrote it, the women who read it, in the nineteenth century

BY HELEN WAITE PAPASHVILY

KENNIKAT PRESS
Port Washington, N. Y./London

ALL THE HAPPY ENDINGS

Copyright © 1956 by Helen Waite Papashvily
Reissued in 1972 by Kennikat Press by arrangement
with Harper & Row, Publishers, Inc.
Library of Congress Catalog Card No: 76-153255
ISBN 0-8046-1497-0

Manufactured by Taylor Publishing Company   Dallas, Texas

ESSAY AND GENERAL LITERATURE INDEX REPRINT SERIES

CONTENTS

ACKNOWLEDGMENTS

My thanks go to the directors and the personnel of all the many libraries I visited while working on this book. I am especially grateful to Mr. James D. Mack, Librarian, Lucy Packer Linderman Library, Lehigh University, and to the members of his staff for the immeasurable help they have given me.

I am also indebted to Mr. Rudolf Hirsch and Mr. Thomas R. Adams, University of Pennsylvania Library; Dr. Lyon N. Richardson, Western Reserve University Library; Dr. Charles A. Anderson, Presbyterian Historical Society, Philadelphia; Mrs. Dorothy Wright, Walter Dexter White Library, California State Polytechnic College, San Luis Obispo; and Miss Florence Garing and Mr. James T. Fitzpatrick, Mercantile Library Association of the City of New York.

Mrs. Dorothy W. Jefferson of the Cecil County Library, Mrs. G. H. Borstel of the Cecil County *Democrat* and Miss Katherine Bratton, all of Elkton, Maryland, aided my search for material about Miss Martha Finley.

In Columbus, Georgia, Miss Loretto Lamar Chappell of The Public Library very kindly found and directed me to sources of information on two early residents of her city, Caroline Lee Hentz and Augusta Evans Wilson. The latter's cousin, Mrs. Anna W. Pease, shared with me her childhood memories of her distinguished relative. Mr. and Mrs. Bentley Chappell and Mrs. Isabel Garrard Patterson were also helpful

Acknowledgments

as were Mr. and Mrs. Douglas Mobley, the present owners of St. Elmo, a home associated with Mrs. Wilson's girlhood.

In Mobile, Alabama, where Mrs. Wilson later lived, I had an opportunity, thanks to Mr. and Mrs. Sidney Phillips, to examine the novelist's correspondence at Kirkbride House and to visit her home, Georgia Cottage, now beautifully restored by Mrs. E. S. Sledge.

At Brockport, New York, Miss Monica Toole showed me the Seymour Library's memorabilia of Mary J. Holmes. Mrs. Jennie Stewart of Fairport, New York, in a long interview recalled many happy memories of her twenty years as the housekeeper for Mr. and Mrs. Holmes.

Mr. R. H. Williams II, Director of the Historical Society of Pennsylvania, allowed me to examine material in its collection and to quote from an unpublished letter of Timothy Shay Arthur.

By permission of Mr. B. E. Powell, Librarian, Duke University Library, I was able to draw extensively from the letters of Mrs. E.D.E.N. Southworth to Robert Bonner. Miss Mattie Russell, Curator of Manuscripts, Duke University Library, gave most generously of her time and information while I was in Durham.

Mr. James W. Patton, Director, Southern Historical Collection, at the University of North Carolina permitted me to include herein extracts from the diaries and letters of Caroline Lee Hentz. The letter of Mrs. Hentz to A. B. Hart, her publisher, is in the Chamberlain Collection of the Boston Public Library. Other letters of Mrs. Hentz, also, came to me through the courtesy of her great-granddaughter, Mrs. Cecil Rhyner.

Acknowledgments

Mr. Edward Morrison in the manuscript room of the New York Public Library called to my attention material pertaining to my subject and I thank the trustees of the Library for permission to quote from letters of Laura Jean Libbey and Ann Stephens.

The late Arthur Rushmore of Harper & Brothers answered many of my questions from his inexhaustible knowledge of the history of bookmaking in the United States.

I am grateful to Dr. Louise Rosenblatt for her constructive criticism of the manuscript.

I have had a wide correspondence with readers of the domestic novel and although limitations of space preclude naming them all here I must mention amusing and perceptive comments by Mrs. Rosette King, Mrs. Joan Younger Dickinson, Mrs. Frederic Starbenz and Mrs. Victor S. Frankenstein.

Like all who write on popular literature, I owe a great debt to James D. Hart's *The Popular Book,* to Frank Luther Mott's *Golden Multitudes* and most especially to Herbert Ross Brown's *The Sentimental Novel in America 1789–1860.* Only Dr. Brown's encouragement coupled with his assurance that he did not intend to carry his definitive study chronologically farther in a future volume emboldened me to attempt this work.

To those I have named, and to many more I have not, I am extremely grateful. Generosity, however, has limits, and some portion of the book—the errors of fact or judgment—I must now claim for myself alone.

Ertoba Farm, Quakertown
Bucks County, Pennsylvania
July 19, 1949—May 20, 1956

xi

FOREWORD

On July 19, 1848, in Seneca Falls, New York, a Woman's Rights Convention, the first ever held, met and after two days of impassioned discussion issued to the press a Declaration of Sentiments beginning:

The history of mankind is a history of repeated injuries and usurpations on the part of man toward woman, having in direct object the establishment of an absolute tyranny over her.

A detailed list of women's grievances followed. Man, the convention charged, had denied woman the franchise, a thorough education, and a chance at the more profitable occupations. He had taken her property and wages, taxed her without representation, made her morally an irresponsible being, usurped the prerogatives of Jehovah Himself over her conscience, and endeavored in every way that he could to destroy her confidence and lessen her self-respect. The assembly at Seneca Falls, determined to correct these injustices by every means possible, concluded on a threatening note:

We shall employ agents, circulate tracts, petition state and national legislatures and endeavor to enlist the pulpit and press in our behalf . . .

Most men reading the accounts of the convention could congratulate themselves and each other on their good luck and good sense in possessing wives and daughters, sisters and mothers who never made such ridiculous accusations or impossible demands but stayed quietly at home content to reign like queens over pretty parlors.

Their dove-eyed darlings, all gentlemen no doubt felt confident, spent *their* leisure as ladies should. They embroidered and painted on velvet and copied verses into albums and pressed leaves and arranged bouquets according to the "language of flowers." At their rosewood pianos they sang and played fashionably pathetic refrains or, reclining on the sofa, they whiled away the time with a sweet novel by Mrs. E.D.E.N. Southworth or Augusta Evans Wilson or Mary J. Holmes or Martha Finley or Marion Harland or some other "scribbling woman."

If a curious husband or father glanced through one of these volumes he found a simple tale of home and family too full of sentiment, sacrifice, devotion and piety perhaps for masculine taste although most suitable and edifying for the female mind.

Throughout the nineteenth century this peculiar literary form, the domestic novel, flourished as never before or since. Hundreds of authors turned out thousands of titles that sold millions of copies. Scarcely a literate woman in the United States but read some of these novels—*The Wide, Wide World, Ishmael; or In the Depths, Tempest and Sunshine, Elsie Dinsmore, St. Elmo, Sunnybank*—to name but a few that in time acquired a kind of subclassic status.

Now these sentimental tales and their authors are almost, if not quite, forgotten by a new generation of readers; accorded only the briefest mention by literary historians, banished from library shelves. Yet such books possess greater value today, perhaps, than when they were written, for in them, as in all popular literature, are mirrored the fears and anxieties and frustrations, the plans and hopes and joys of those who read them so avidly. Their crumbling pages reveal the dream world of women—as it existed in the nineteenth century and lingered on to influence the twentieth.

The domestic or, according to its critics, the sentimental novel was in general what the terms imply—a tale of contemporary domestic life, ostensibly sentimental in tone and with few exceptions almost always written by women for women. This and a certain similarity in the binding style, "large, handsome duodecimo, cloth, gilt," would seem, at first glance, to be all many of the domestic novels had in common.

Some, in their gory sensationalism, rivaled the old ballad sheets and chap books while others, oozing sanctimonious piety, imitated tracts. Quite often, to avoid even the slightest taint of fiction, these novels bore as subtitles, "A True History," "Founded on Fact," "Drawn from Incidents in Real Life," or appeared disguised as diaries, memoirs, journals, collections of letters, autobiographies, or some similar form of eyewitness account by an innocent bystander.

A few of the authors wrote merely to amuse; more hoped to do that and at the same time plead a special cause or share their convictions on a variety of controversial subjects. Several of the domestic novelists had real talent, imagination and skill and one possessed true genius. Those who did not borrowed from their contemporaries and predecessors, thereby proving the feminine knack with leftovers as useful in the library as in the kitchen. A Richardson heroine, a Brontë hero, bits of pathos and drollery out of Dickens, a seasoning of supernatural horrors from Mrs. Radcliffe or Monk Lewis mixed well and liberally garnished with local color could be served up as original concoctions.

Yet, despite their varied form, basically the domestic novels were ever the same. The center of interest was the home although that edifice might range from one of Mrs. E.D.E.N. Southworth's noble English castles to the tastefully adorned wigwam of Malaeska in Mrs. Ann Stephens' book of the same name. The common woman was always glorified, her every thought, action, gesture, chance word fraught with esoteric meaning and far-reaching influence; her daily routine of cooking, washing, baking, nursing, scrubbing imbued with dramatic significance; her petty trials and small joys magnified to heroic proportions.

There were no historical figures, few excursions into the past or the future. Their own world and the immediate present occupied readers and writers exclusively.

The authors of the domestic novel shared curiously similar backgrounds. Almost all were women of upper-middle-class origin who began very early in life to write, frequently under pressure of sudden poverty. Several published while still in their teens (usually a temperance tale). A majority lived or visited in the South. Most important for many of these women, somewhere, sometime, someplace in her past some man—a father, a brother, a husband, a guardian—had proved unworthy of the trust and confidence she placed in him. This traumatic experience, never resolved, grew into a chronic grievance.

The small crimes of men—their propensity to make noise and dirt and war and trouble—the insensitivity, the violence, the lust inherent in the masculine character might sometimes be overlooked, but readers and writers and their unifying symbol, the heroines, could never forget how a man boasted and swaggered and threatened and promised and commanded —nor ever forgive that in the end he failed.

No man, fortunately for his peace of mind, ever discovered that the domestic novels were handbooks of another kind of feminine revolt—that these pretty tales reflected and encouraged a pattern of feminine behavior so quietly ruthless, so subtly vicious that by comparison the ladies at Seneca appear angels of innocence.

Even so astute an observer as Vernon K. Parrington could dismiss the sentimental novel as weak "cambric tea." Like the rest of his sex, he did not detect the faint bitter taste of poison in the cup nor recognize that these books were rather a witches' broth, a lethal draught brewed by women and used by women to destroy their common enemy, man.

It is not to be imagined that the ways and means of correcting a long list of feminine grievances were communicated on a conscious level. The link between reader and writer forged by every popular book is a mystic one. The writer may not know all he has said; the reader all he has heard; yet they understand each other perfectly.

Nineteenth-century women, if they were to achieve freedom in what seemed to them a hostile world, needed direction, inspiration, appreciation, reassurance, a sense of self-importance and of group unity, a plan of action.

The Seneca Falls Convention supplied this to a few women but uncounted hundreds and thousands more found *their* Declaration of Rights, *their* Statement of Intentions within the pages of the domestic novel.

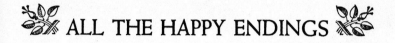 ALL THE HAPPY ENDINGS

1 🌿 All Women—
All Enchained—All Enchanted

Iɴ ᴛʜᴇ summer of 1850, Mr. George P. Putnam, a
New York bookseller and publisher, was waited upon by
a gentleman who wished to submit a novel, or, as he preferred calling it, "a story," the first his daughter had ever
written.

The manuscript was well thumbed and more than slightly
dog-eared, for it had been read and rejected by almost every
other publisher in New York.

Mr. Putnam, left to himself, might have concurred in the
general opinion but something in the title (which as a matter
of fact had nothing whatever to do with the text) struck him,
he later said, "as fresh and uncommon" and he carried the
book, *The Wide, Wide World* by Elizabeth Wetherell, home
to Staten Island.

His mother, Mrs. Catherine Putnam, was visiting him
and he gave her the manuscript.

"See," he said, "if it is worth publishing."

Mrs. Putnam read through the pile of handwritten pages
and returned an immediate verdict.

"If you never publish another book, George, publish this!"

Mr. Putnam took her advice and, although the season was

rather advanced, made plans to issue the volume in time for the Christmas trade. In doing this the publisher acted solely on his mother's judgment, for not then, nor in galley sheets, nor presumably at any time thereafter did Mr. Putnam ever read and judge for himself the merits of *The Wide, Wide World*.

Late in December, 1850, the book was ready. Sales, to Mr. Putnam's discouragement, were a little slow the first week. Again his mother pronounced in the book's behalf. Providence, she assured her son, would aid him.

Mrs. Putnam believed in mystical signs, in portents, in the double meaning of spiritual symbolism, so perhaps she was not surprised when almost immediately an enthusiastic review of the book appeared in a Providence (R.I.) newspaper and a large order from a Providence bookseller followed.

Within two weeks after publication the Boston and New York critics had discovered *The Wide, Wide World* and joined in a chorus of praise.

". . . one book like this is not produced in an age," said the *New York Times*.

The first edition sold out in four months. Available copies commanded a premium until Putnam's printed a second edition and then a third, a fourth, a fifth, on and on until eventually *The Wide, Wide World* achieved a sale unsurpassed by any previous novel.

Translations appeared in France, Germany, Sweden and Italy. In England the book had a reception unequaled by any previous American novel. "The author," said the Edinburgh *Witness*, "has few equals and no superiors on either side of the Atlantic."

All Women—All Enchained—All Enchanted

Even Charles Darwin's daughter, her niece remembered long after, read *The Wide, Wide World* aloud to the family "with all the religion and deaths from consumption left out and all the good country food left in."

At home, six "lyrical passages" from the text were set to music and the title became a catch phrase. Shocked, but perhaps slightly flattered, too, the author noted in her diary the advertisement of a New York store: "In the 'Wide, Wide World' cannot be found better undergarments than at James E. Rays, 108 Bowery."

The simple tale had universal appeal. The Newark *Daily Advertiser* spoke for the pious when it declared "The Wide, Wide World is capable of doing more good than any other work, other than the Bible." Eventually the worldly had to read it, too, just because, as Mrs. George Bancroft, the wife of the historian, complained to a friend, it *was* the fashion.

Letters of praise from great and humble, from friend and stranger came to the author's desk, for it did not long remain a secret that Elizabeth Wetherell was the pen name of Susan Warner, the daughter of Henry Warner, a once-successful and prominent New York lawyer.

Long before Putnam's accepted *The Wide, Wide World* and it was still making the rounds of the New York publishers, an editor at Harper's (fortunately for his professional reputation nameless) rejected the manuscript with a caustic "Fudge!" penciled on one sheet. Confronted with the book's subsequent popularity he must have spent many puzzled hours trying to determine wherein lay the secret appeal he had overlooked. The modern reader is in much the same quandary.

The book, almost devoid of plot, told the story of Ellen

3

Montgomery, a lachrymose, pious, hypersensitive orphan sent to live with unknown relatives in the country.

The author had small interest in children. Almost cruelly indifferent to her adoring sister, Anna, eight years her junior, until both were well into womanhood, Susan Warner did not know or want to know young people.

While visiting her publisher she wrote home:

> None of the Putnam children appear at breakfast or tea and I like that very well I must say. What possibility of conversation is there at a table where four or five children are to be attended to?

A compliment the young Putnams reciprocated in later life by remembering Miss Warner as "a kind of giant with a long head swaying on a long neck."

Ellen Montgomery consequently was not a very appealing little girl. Ungrateful to the aunt who gave her a home, condescending to her simple old grandmother and to her aunt's betrothed, because he was "a common farmer," she performed her share of household tasks with little skill and less grace and her religious activity ran more to preaching than to practice. A spiritual and social snob, nevertheless she won the affection of all about her, the heart of a handsome, wellborn clergyman, the fortune of a dour Scotch uncle, and the interest of a million readers.

Novelty accounted for some of this great popularity. *The Wide, Wide World* was one of the first real, full-length novels authority or conscience permitted many to enjoy.

Tracts in quantity masqueraded as fiction, but the activities and eventual fortunes of Miss Lazy and Master Greedy predestined from the first page provided little drama or suspense. A number of magazines carried short stories; booksellers, beginning as early as 1680, imported the newest romances from abroad; Benjamin Franklin's publication of Samuel Richardson's *Pamela* in 1744 attracted so many readers (and pennies of profit) that thereafter reprints of fiction appeared wherever presses turned; between 1770 and 1850 nearly fourteen hundred works of fiction by native authors were published in the United States.

Yet, despite all this, fiction in general remained suspect, condemned by divines, schoolmasters, editors, all the sober and sensible, on the grounds it encouraged indolence and dissatisfaction if not outright immorality.

Perhaps because the temptation was so great and so constant, and the gratification so easy and so delightful, novel reading came to be one of the great battlegrounds of conscience in the nineteenth century. Again and again diaries and letters of the period record the soul struggles of readers who succumbed to fiction one day and repented their indulgence the next.

Susan Warner's own diary is full of poignant examples of this conflict that beset so many others.

Foolishly enough, I got engaged in Helen. I read a long while and what was the consequence . . . I just got down to breakfast from my thoughts. Oh, how wretched it is to do so; I hate it. And yet scarcely struggle against it.

But who could resist? Soon she fell again.

Stood up by my gas light after Anna was in bed, reading in The Initials till quite late—and got into bed sorry and sorry for my self-indulgence and wrong doing.

5

Susan Warner disliked having the word "novel" applied to her work; she preferred "stories" or "books." With further self-contradiction, Ellen Montgomery in *The Wide, Wide World* was forbidden to read *Blackwood's Magazine* since it contained fiction and when her future husband departed for a space of years he exacted her promise that she would read no novels in his absence.

The appearance of *The Wide, Wide World* changed this attitude. The church sanctioned the work by making it a standard item like *Pilgrim's Progress* and Foxe's *Book of Martyrs* for Sunday-school libraries. Troubled consciences might be eased also by the thought that Professor William Gammell, the eminent critic and theologian, declared Miss Warner: ". . . has succeeded I think better than any other writer in our language in making religious sentiments appear natural and attractive in a story that possesses the interest of romance."

The pious tone of Susan Warner's novel, the Bible references, the round of hymn singing and soul searching punctuated by happy deathbeds, repentant sinners and frequent conversions won acceptance for the more secular portions of the work, and these were many—the romance, the descriptions of travel, the accounts of parties and social life at home and abroad, the details of costumes and furnishings. The author had a good eye for the American scene—not for Cooper's wild forests or Irving's fanciful glens, but for the everyday world, particularly as women knew it—winter fields streaked with pale sun and long shadows, new snow on a dead garden, hot summer middays still and lovely, tanglewoods, stone-fenced fields, elm-arched roads linking farms to towns, "full of the

6

buzz of business," their streets lined with "marble emporiums" where supercilious clerks displayed nankeens and fine merinos. "I love to read about good eating," Susan Warner once said. She wrote about that, too. Not only the Darwins liked the pickling, preserving, baking and sausage making that filled the pages. Readers often wrote Susan Warner that *The Wide, Wide World* had saved souls, it apparently whetted appetites as well, for many begged "the receipts for the biscuit on which the cat set his paw"; for "splitters," "for the cake Alice made."

Formal balls and apple-cutting bees, music lessons and buttermaking, Susan Warner knew the daily life of women, rich, poor and middle class, in town and in the country. Their duties and their pleasures, their daring extravagances, their small economies were part of her own experience and she could imbue commonplace events and incidents with dramatic interest.

Anyone who ever read *The Wide, Wide World* (and that includes almost all literate females native born in the nineteenth century) usually remembers two scenes of special charm, and perhaps it is these unforgettable bits in a book, rather than any over-all excellence, that makes the classic, major or minor.

Early in *The Wide, Wide World* Ellen's dying mother bought her a mahogany desk. She and Ellen, and the reader with them, lingered over the fittings, everything that might be to Ellen's use or advantage when the invalid was gone— they selected letter paper, large and small, with envelopes and note sheets to match, an inkstand, steel and quill pens, a little ivory knife and a leaf cutter, sealing waxes in red,

7

green, blue and yellow, lights, wafers, a seal, a paper folder, a pounce box, a ruler, a neat silver pencil, drawing pencils, India rubber, and sheets of drawing paper.

Many readers have confessed that yearning over these delightful objects they quite missed the intended poignancy and would have counted a mother well lost for such a desk gained.

Another of the book's memorable scenes described a holiday party where Ellen and some other children, their eyes hidden, drew for coveted pieces of leather in purple, scarlet, rose, green, blue.

To make sure of an especially beautiful bit of morocco, Ellen peeked. Later, troubled by conscience, she confessed the crime and won the admiration of the entire company, since then, as now, an acknowledgment of dishonesty seemed more praiseworthy than honesty itself.

Beyond the handsome desk, the pretty morocco bits, however, few readers can go. They remember only that all through the book little Ellen wept and they wept with her— on page after page their tears fell together. Yet strangely no one can recall just why—except it was sad—*so* sad—so *very* sad.

In reality there was nothing in *The Wide, Wide World* to cause this contagious, almost epidemic, melancholia—no Oliver Twists, or Little Nells pulled at the heartstrings; no slums or workhouses or charity schools pricked a tender conscience.

Ellen lost her home and parents, but literary convention had made that customary, if not obligatory, for heroines of the period. Her aunt was rather sharp tongued; she boxed Ellen's ears; she dyed her white stockings brown; she withheld a letter, but Ellen always had an unfailing champion in her aunt's betrothed, Mr. Van Brunt, and when not basking in his rather fatuous admiration she visited among a circle of admiring friends who showered upon her innumerable gifts ranging from a tastefully bound *Pilgrim's Progress* to a spirited pony.

For an era when cold rooms, Spartan fare and hard beds were thought to function as character builders and the most devoted parents showed concern for their children's welfare in strict discipline and harsh punishments, Ellen fared far better than many of her contemporaries in fact or fiction.

In 1865 little Rudyard Kipling and his younger sister, Mary, were left, like Miss Warner's heroine, in the care of relatives when their parents returned to India. Beaten, bullied, starved and tortured by *their* aunt, mystified by *their* parents' desertion, the little Kiplings read *The Wide, Wide World* and understandably found no help in its pages for their own real tragedy, no kinship, as Mary Kipling wrote, with "that seepy-weepy Ellen Montgomery."

This seepy-weepiness provoked frequent outbursts of masculine scorn, very often editorially expressed, but to no avail. Neither criticism, satire nor parody could diminish the book's appeal or silence the chorus of feminine readers sobbing with Ellen Montgomery as she fell into a brook, presided at a deathbed, made a mistake in drawing, heard a hymn, burned a cake, watched the sun go down or thought of the unconverted.

Ellen was far from the first heroine to set the tears flowing. Goethe's *Sorrows of Werther* in 1774 started the style abroad and beginning in 1789 with the very first American novel, William H. Brown's *The Power of Sympathy,* a maze of incestuous passion, unrequited love, seduction and mass suicide, the school of sensibility flourished at home. Yet just why readers, mostly women, took such morbid pleasure in crying over declines and deathbeds, sepulchers and cemeteries, no one attempted to explain.

There are no "idle tears." The stylized horrors of Brown and his successors, the petty trials of Ellen Montgomery, but substituted for real and persistent grievances and if a reader could not always give them name or form, nevertheless she wept like Ellen because "all the scattered causes of sorrow . . . were gathered together and pressing upon her at once."

What were these "scattered sorrows" that pressed so heavily on the heroine and drew such an immediate response from the reader? To understand them one must know something of the author, of her readers and of the world they lived in.

It was no accident that Publisher Putnam's mother, Catherine Palmer Putnam recognized qualities in *The Wide, Wide World* that all the masculine editors in New York missed. By a strange coincidence the magic of a best seller had touched Mrs. Putnam before. As a girl she attended the school kept by Mrs. Susanna Rowson, the author of *Charlotte Temple,* a novel published originally in England in 1791 and more frequently reprinted in the United States than any other work of fiction until *The Wide, Wide World* appeared.

Mrs. Rowson certainly knew and, in one of her later novels, *The Inquisitor,* listed exactly what attracted readers—"a sufficient quantity of sighs, tears, swooning, hysterics and moving expressions of heart rending woe"—but it is doubtful if she passed the formula on to her students. More probably Catherine Putnam sensed *The Wide, Wide World's* appeal because she and the author and the tremendous audience who wept over the pages for more than half a century shared a common lot. In a world made for men they were women. Law, custom and theology told them they were inferior. Experience proved to them that they were not. Day after day, year after year women lived within the frustrating confines of this contradiction, and gathered "scattered sorrows," reasons to weep, from injustices they could not understand and customs they could not change.

Catherine Putnam married very young, perhaps before she was sixteen. Almost immediately thereafter her husband's health mysteriously failed. His affliction precluded any indoor work, eventually any work at all. "For soon," to quote his son, "he found himself fascinated with outdoor life with the result of becoming diverted from his legal work." His wife fortunately had courage and, thanks to Mrs. Rowson, a good education. She opened a school and from then on supported her husband and their five children.

Susan Warner, the author of *The Wide, Wide World*, lived through a similar experience. When she was born in 1819 in New York her father, advancing rapidly in the legal profession, practiced both in town and before the court in Albany and provided his family, in the language of the period, with "a home of elegance and refinement." Susan and her younger sister, Anna, enjoyed all the luxuries of the day—new books by Sir Walter Scott and Miss Edgeworth, pictures by Murillo and Sir Joshua Reynolds, a piano, lessons in music and French and Italian, concerts, botanizing expeditions, parties and dresses of India muslin and slippers in scarlet leather to wear to them.

When his daughters were young ladies Mr. Warner bought

Constitution Island in the Hudson River, just off West Point, for a summer home and planned a suitable mansion with gardens to adorn it. Almost at once difficulties arose over title to the island and the validity of some resales Mr. Warner made and in the difficulties that followed, a tangle of verbal contracts, protracted lawsuits, disappearing witnesses and false friends, Mr. Warner lost not only his fortune but the initiative to recoup it as well.

The family had to give up their gay life in town, "among crimson cushions and tall mirrors, with greenhouse and carriages and a corps of servants close at hand," as Anna Warner wrote afterwards in a biography of her sister, Susan. They took refuge on Constitution Island in an old Revolutionary War dwelling originally intended for the caretaker.

Affairs grew progressively worse and, although through the kindness of friends Mr. Warner retained the island, all the family's possessions excepting only the barest necessities, went to pay his debts.

Anna Warner described the sad day:

When we had watched our little Sir Joshua as long as we could see it and given farewell touches to my sister's piano and followed with our hearts the many precious books and engravings, when at last the men and the confusion were gone; then we woke up to life. . . .

Without training, experience or advice Susan and Anna Warner began the task of supporting themselves, their father and their aunt. This was the common road that led many other women to authorship during the nineteenth century.

As Anna Warner remembered:

Aunt Fanny stood washing up the cups and saucers while my sister was near by towel in hand . . . the room was very still and full of thoughts. Then Aunt Fanny spoke, "Sue, I believe if you would try, you could write a story" whether she added "that would sell" I'm not sure but of course that was what she meant.

My sister made no answer. But as she finished wiping the dishes and went back and forth to put them away, the first dim far off notion of The Wide, Wide World came into her head . . . I think the opening words were written that very night.

Thereafter, although these girls (for Anna turned author, too) earned the money that supported the family, their father had the spending of it. In consequence they lived always on the edge of poverty. The returns from *The Wide, Wide World* alone might have provided a lifetime of comfort. Mr. Warner poured that and everything else his daughters received into his unsuccessful projects and needed still more money.

Susan and Anna had to forgo the more profitable royalty payments for their work and sell the copyrights for immediate cash. They wrote juveniles, short stories, articles, and books for which they often had little heart. They attempted a magazine; they corrected papers; arranged dictation books for teachers; prepared Sunday-school lessons—it was still not enough—they raised and sold vegetables.

Not only did their father's poor management swallow their income but his indecision hampered their lives. They could make no plans on their own. If they wished to know his plans for them, it required a prearranged line of conversation and considerable diplomacy to lead him to reveal them. Men, competent or not, ruled the world.

Mrs. Putnam and the Warner sisters, ladies at Seneca and ladies at home each in her own way had endured and resented masculine domination.

On February 23, 1859, Susan Warner wrote in her diary:

Got into the cooler little back room and rested with a charming little talk with Mrs. Hutton about her reading The Wide, Wide World in her kitchen to her black woman and Irish woman and two little children—all enchained.

The smaller difference of religion, color, nationality, age class, culture pattern were forgotten—all women—all enchanted—all enchained. How to be free, that was now the question.

2 ❧ The Revolt—
Active and Passive

THE AGITATION for woman's rights did not begin, of course, with the Seneca Falls convention.

As early as 1776, while the Constitution was in the making, Abigail Adams wrote to her husband, John:

I desire you would remember the ladies and be more favorable to them than your ancestors. Do not put such unlimited power into the hands of husbands. Remember all men would be tyrants if they could. If particular care and attention are not paid to the ladies, we are determined to foment a rebellion and will not hold ourselves bound to obey any laws in which we have no voice or representation.

A few churches, notably the Society of Friends, and many distinguished individuals, Thomas Paine, Ralph Waldo Emerson, William Ellery Channing, Margaret Fuller Ossoli among them, urged women be given more opportunities in education, the trades and professions, greater equality before the law, and the right to vote.

The Seneca convention *did* make the issue of Woman's Rights more acute. As they had threatened, the ladies pleaded their cause from the pulpit, the lecture platform and the newspapers, to be answered almost immediately by the opposition.

Each group (and no sex lines were drawn, men and women rallied to both sides) drew upon theology, philosophy, tradition and biology to prove their points; each illustrated their argument with lurid stories full of sensational detail which ensured listeners if not adherents to their respective causes.

Those who advocated more rights for women justified their demands by presenting documented particulars of wife beaters, child killers, seducers, debauchers and drunkards, tales of men who mistreated their wives physically and mentally, were unfaithful to their marriage vows and brought the proof of this infidelity home to infect their families. They told of monsters who drove helpless women to insanity and death, and still unsatisfied, carried their persecutions beyond the grave and appropriated their widow's property, ignored her children and, the worst crime of all, replaced her with a younger, more attractive, successor.

The opponents of the women's parties countered with equally well-authenticated cases of heartless, cruel females, coquettes, schemers and parasites—wives whose extravagances led to bankruptcy, their follies to dishonor. They described noble men tied forever to indolent, stupid, ill or unsympathetic mates, of heroes sacrificed to faults and vices not their own—their lot more tragic than the most ill-treated woman's, for men, being morally and legally responsible for their wives' behavior, lived in a double jeopardy.

The two parties went on matching case against case (and on occasion still do so) without convincing each other or arriving anywhere near the truth.

For, although the question appeared to be a simple one for which there might be simple, if diametrically opposed answers, it was not, and the obscure and complex nature of the issue may be discerned only by re-examining the effect of the Industrial Revolution on the lives of women and men.

The changes in the work pattern of men, the emotional and physical adjustment required of them when they moved from the simpler forms of production to the machine are fairly well known if, even yet, hardly comprehended. The impact of the Industrial Revolution upon the life of the family with particular reference to women is less well understood.

When production centered in the home all women, the rich and the poor, had a share in it. Certain well-defined and relatively specialized duties were traditionally theirs and so, too, were the privileges and perquisites that went with them. This does not mean women enjoyed complete equality. They did not. They did have, and quite apart from their childbearing role, an acknowledged position as skilled technicians.

When the machine came, the center of production shifted from the home and farm to the factory and men followed. As the feminine trades, baking, brewing, tailoring, weaving, spinning, to name a few, gradually became commercial enterprises, poor women had two choices—stay at home, deprived of their old gainful employment, and let the labor of one wage earner support four, eight, perhaps a dozen people or leave their children and, like their men, go out of their homes to work.

There was no lack of opportunity for those who wished to take the latter course. The mills from the very beginning welcomed women willing to spin sixteen hours a day; the mines offered them a chance to drag coal carts underground.

17

But to what advantage? Neither prestige nor cash was theirs. The old privileges had vanished and the man of the house had a legal right to the wages earned by his family.

The rest of the female population fared little better than their poorer sisters. A few centuries before the Industrial Revolution the chatelaine of a castle was its business manager —the executive in charge of production—expected and able to provision and outfit her husband and his troops for a pilgrimage or a campaign, manage the fief in his absence, practice medicine, dispense justice and, as a sideline, play the lute, compose verse, complete a tapestry and educate her daughters to do likewise.

The Industrial Revolution created a different kind of upper class and a whole new middle class. Surplus wealth increased, but it no longer took the old form of landed property which demanded many feminine skills for its proper development and maintenance and rewarded the possessors of these skills proportionately.

In the new economy profits went into stocks and bonds, commercial and industrial ventures. Women lacked the training and experience to share in the management of these possessions and they were strictly prohibited from acquiring either by a new taboo.

For when wealth no longer took the form of castles and granaries, sweeping fields and wide timberlands, flocks and herds, men needed other symbols to indicate their prosperity. The first and most important sign of success came to be the idle woman in the household. She, like the ornaments which adorned and surrounded her, offered proof that some man had achieved so great a surplus he could afford objects not only for use but for waste.

The pattern evolved slowly. The changes in the life of any individual were few and imperceptible and women, at least in the European countries and the British Isles, passively accepted their new role with little protest. Not until too late did they realize that responsibilities and rights are indivisible. To relinquish one is to lose both.

In the United States quite a different situation developed. The speed at which the Industrial Revolution proceeded, the pattern it followed, was not constant but varied greatly between political and geographical areas. Nowhere was this more clearly evinced than in early colonial America. Here each new family, each new community meeting the frontier, met also, as far as physical conditions were concerned, the world as it existed before the Industrial Revolution, but— and herein was the core of the confusion—they met it with a psychology, an ideology, a legal system derived from societies several generations into the Industrial Revolution.

For women this meant a resumption of their old pre-Industrial Revolution position and their old prestige—at least for a time, and the letters, diaries and newspapers of the eighteenth century show women busy in a variety of careers. They kept taverns and shops and managed farms; they manufactured, processed and traded; they spun and wove; they made lace, dyed silk and bleached linen; they were printers, editors, teachers, doctors, nurses, druggists and writers. They won respect and admiration from their masculine contemporaries and, better than either, the right to conduct their own affairs. In three states, no law indicating the contrary, women even voted.

Then came the inevitable machine and with it, as always, centralized production. When the shop, the office, the factory moved out of the home women lost their chance for vocational and professional training and business experience. The trades came to require more specialized techniques, the professions greater academic knowledge, than women could acquire at home. As new laws were passed and older ones more strictly enforced, women found their opportunities further curtailed.

In settlement after settlement as the frontier moved west and south the same thing happened and sometimes very quickly. For economic history, repeating itself, gained momentum in the process and a decade in the New World often accomplished the social changes of a century in the Old.

As each new community grew and expanded and what seemed a divinely ordained prosperity followed, the lady was needed again to symbolize masculine success. A woman might accept the new role, but not the restrictions that went with it. Her European great-grandmother had conceded the superiority of the male in all things because she lacked within the span of her own life any experience to indicate the contrary.

To convince an American woman was not so simple. At twenty-five, perhaps, she had crossed a wilderness, raised a cabin, brained a panther, outwitted an Indian, improvised a corn sheller, set a broken leg, brought in a crop, and traded a setting of eggs into a dairy herd. At fifty such a woman must have laughed in her fan or her subconscious when gentlemen solemnly declared the female constitution would collapse under the strain of voting, managing money or studying for a profession.

In addition to the social and economic contradictions in their new society, the American colonists labored under a peculiar and anomalous legal system. The early settlers had brought along English common law as their basic code. Like most travelers, however, they left something important forgotten at home, in this case a Court of Chancery to function as a judicial balance.

Common law, at least according to Blackstone, whose *Commentaries* came to be regarded in the young Republic not as an interpretation but as the law itself, held that husband and wife were one in the husband which gave a married woman few rights before the law and almost no control over her person, her property and her children.

It was little help to an American woman that Blackstone's compatriots considered him inaccurate and prejudiced or that common law in England was frequently modified by the Chancery Court, which exercised special control over the settlements, dower rights, and private property of women and often rendered extremely favorable decisions in their behalf.

An aggrieved wife in the United States appealing for redress to a village squire or a county judge whose library usually held the Bible, Blackstone and the state statutes, based on common law based in turn on Blackstone, was at a decided disadvantage.

Like many legal conceptions, the control of husband over wife was modified, of course, in actual practice. Individual women by various and traditional methods achieved equality and even domination in the marriage relationship. Henpecked husbands, then as now, served as the butt of jokes. In a really intolerable situation a wife, though it meant a great loss of feminine face, could rely on the pressure of public opinion to alleviate her lot.

Nevertheless, until almost the middle of the nineteenth century, marriage, as circumscribed by statute and court decisions and social custom, was essentially a master-slave tie, based, like all such relationships, upon the implied if unspoken covenant that the weaker surrenders body and will in return for care and protection from the stronger, whose superior intelligence, power or ability guarantees the bond.

Perhaps under certain conditions, given a patriarchal society, small, isolated, closely integrated, with a static economy and rigid system of taboos, it might be possible to maintain the fiction of masculine omnipotence. There, if one man fails, another, a husband, father or brother, stands ready to assume the obligation.

In the rushing, bustling, shifting world of nineteenth-century America, this was impossible. The revolutions, both political and industrial, mass immigration, rapid urbanization, the special hazards of the frontier changed the social structure of the family and made new demands on the individual.

Many a woman accepted the conditions of the old covenant and her inferiority cheerfully and unquestioningly, abided faithfully by her part of the bargain only to find herself alone, her life and perhaps her children's dependent on her unaided effort. It is not important whether this happened because a good husband died or a bad one deserted, because an ocean or a continent barred a father's or a brother's help, the failure nullified the moral contract.

The untenable premise of masculine superiority not only victimized women—men suffered, too. Contrary to the agitators for and against woman's rights, few husbands were heartless brutes, few wives heedless imbeciles, and most

22

couples avoided the extremes of conduct legally permitted under the marriage contract. Yet, even so, they still had to tolerate its norm, to endure the anxieties, frustrations, doubts and inefficiencies inherent in a relationship where at all times and in all situations one partner must direct all action and assume all responsibility and the other, despite equal or superior ability pertinent to the occasion, render compliance or practice deceit.

Some women, the ladies at Seneca Falls and their converts, for example, would accept neither of these alternatives. They brought their revolt into the open; they defied convention and irate husbands and fathers; they spoke out boldly for their rights or what they believed to be their rights. They wrote and argued and worked for goals they felt would assure them greater happiness. The goals sometimes proved disappointing and the methods used to achieve them often foolish or futile, occasionally illegal and violent, but they *were* overt. What the feminists wanted and the lengths they would go to achieve their ends were only too well known to all who would stop to listen.

These vociferous women, however, rallied but a small minority to their cause. At its peak the suffrage movement had the active support of less than 10 per cent of the women in the United States.

Meantime what of the other 90 per cent, the quiet, docile, inarticulate women at home? Were they satisfied with the world about them and their place in it? Was their deepest concern with dress and fashion and gossip? Were they so grateful for a husband and children that they were content to have them on poor terms rather than not at all?

23

Most of the historians and sociologists of the period felt sure that women, "good" women at least, found their lot ideal. By the last decade of the nineteenth century a growing school of psychologists concurred in this opinion. Active feminists, said these learned gentlemen, are a strange kind of monster, unsexed by their envy of men. The "real" womanly woman is quiet, placid and acquiescent, for submission, the wish and need to be dominated, is inherent in the female organism.

No one questioned the amateur biology involved nor asked why, in all animal life, this quality should be found in one species only, homo sapiens. Few, indeed, noted that the historians, sociologists and psychologists who set down these definitive laws were, by a not so strange coincidence, men.

Men, it seemed, could conceive of no revolt, no resistance, without overt action. Yet there was dissatisfaction and a determination for change among women who did not carry banners or march in parades or speak in public. Some, no doubt, traded grievances and the remedies for them with their friends and neighbors and relatives; a few recorded their complaints in diaries, letters and journals; most women however kept a ladylike silence. Perhaps they lacked words and phrases to protest the inequalities and injustices they felt, perhaps they knew open defiance of masculine authority seldom succeeded.

Nonetheless the quiet women revolted, too, and waged their own devious, subtle, undeclared war against men—their manual of arms, their handbook of strategy was the sentimental domestic novel they read for half a century. The pages reveal the tactics women adopted, the weapons they chose, the victories they sought—and finally won.

3 🌿 The Rise
of the Fallen

THE FIRST half century of American independence accomplished political emancipation from England, but the bonds of literary servitude were not so easily severed.

"In the four quarters of the globe who reads an American book?" Sydney Smith scornfully asked in 1820. American shelves full of Fielding, Defoe, Richardson, Smollett, Sterne, Scott, Maria Edgeworth, Jane Porter and Mrs. Radcliffe answered his question. Between 1779 and 1829 native authors produced scarcely more than two hundred works of fiction— most of which lived and died with their first audience. Of this total and of the twenty-odd titles that did achieve any real circulation better than a third were written for or by women. In subject, form and characterization they followed British models.

Eighteenth-century England offered little choice in dramatic theme for those who wished to write about women. A female figure might, of course, be draped in historical trappings or propelled through the horrors of a Gothic romance, but a man could serve the same purpose as well or better. The novelist who attempted to show a real woman living in a real world, one acting in accord with the accepted sex pattern of the period, faced several problems in literary craftsmanship.

The matron had no story of her own. She existed in the shadow of her husband. The conventions surrounding the unmarried girl restricted her participation in the world and centered her struggle for existence around a single goal—a husband. An occasional novel explored some other aspect of feminine life but the brutal realism of Defoe in *Moll Flanders* and *Roxana*, the astringent satire of Jane Austen, the sensibility of Richardson and the efforts of a host of lesser writers were all expended in resolving the same problem—will the woman succeed in achieving the marriage which she seeks more eagerly than does the man?

The earliest American novels about women continued in this same tradition. In fact two of the most popular, *Charlotte Temple* and *Rebecca, Fille de Chambre*, were originally published in England. Their author, Susanna Haswell Rowson, an early example of the "American career woman," enjoyed a kind of dual citizenship. Born in England in 1762, Susanna Haswell was left in the care of relatives after her mother's early death and her father's emigration to America. When she was five her father, who had established a new home and a new family in the colonies, returned to England for Susanna. After an exceedingly perilous voyage, a shipwreck off Long Island and a rescue which the embryo author survived (and utilized twenty-five years later in her novel *Rebecca*), the pair arrived in Boston.

Susanna's father had the means and the inclination to give his daughter a better education than most young women received. She became proficient in music, rhetoric and the classics, often reciting from Homer and Virgil for the edification, and perhaps amazement, of her father's guests.

These talents remained parlor ornaments until Mr. Haswell's Tory sentiments, too openly expressed during the Revolution, led to the confiscation of his estates. Penniless, the family fled to England. There Susanna's "advantages," fortified by her native spirit, wit and intelligence, procured her a place as governess in the household of the Duchess of Devonshire who was a friend of Sheridan, Fox, Samuel Johnson, Fanny Burney and something of bluestocking herself. Encouraged by so influential a patron, the young governess began to write and soon had to her credit a volume of poetry and four novels, *Victoria* in 1786, *The Inquisitor* in 1788, *Mary; or, the Test of Honour* in 1789, and *Charlotte Temple* in 1791. Her books brought her some profit in cash though more in favorable notice which she quickly utilized by making her presentation to the Prince of Wales an opportunity to beg a pension for her father. About this time, perhaps at court, Susanna met and married William Rowson, a prosperous hardware merchant who also served as bandmaster in the Royal Guards.

Almost immediately thereafter Rowson's business failed and to his economic liabilities were added some moral ones. He drank excessively and he had an illegitimate son. Mrs. Rowson assumed the care of this child and of her husband's young sister and set to work to support the family by writing two more books: *Mentoria*, a volume of advice to young ladies, and *Rebecca, Fille de Chambre*, a semiautobiographical novel. When the returns on these proved insufficient for the family's needs, Mrs. Rowson found places for herself and her husband in a provincial theatrical troupe. This disbanding, the Rowsons accepted an offer from the manager of a

Philadelphia company to come to the United States. For the next three years the couple played in theaters along the seaboard while off stage Mrs. Rowson adapted plays, arranged music and wrote songs to order.

By 1794, the year after her arrival in Philadelphia, American editions of *The Inquisitor, Rebecca* and *Charlotte Temple* had appeared. The two latter books found a far more receptive audience here than in England.

Mrs. Rowson's fame grew. She wrote some original plays— perhaps the first woman to do so in the new Republic—a comedy, a tragedy, a musical farce and an opera. When William Cobbett satirized one of her adaptations, she turned the tables by satirizing his satire in a novel and had the honor of adding Lady Washington's name to the subscribers for the book, *Trials of the Human Heart.*

In 1797, after several months at the Federal Theatre in Boston, Mrs. Rowson retired to open a fashionable school for girls near the city. Here, where Catherine Palmer Putnam was a pupil, Mrs. Rowson taught "the common branches" as well as "embroiderie, geography and musicke," providing for the latter accomplishment one of the very first pianos in the country and an instructor to explain its mysteries.

Mrs. Rowson made an excellent teacher. Eliza Bowne, one of her students, described her as "an amiable lady, so mild, so good no one can help loving her. She treats all her scholars with such a tenderness as would win the affection of the most savage brute."

Her theatrical past proved no barrier to success; nor did her advanced ideas on woman's rights and abolition. At the end of her first year she had one hundred pupils and a long waiting list.

In addition to her school duties Mrs. Rowson found time to support several charitable and philanthropic causes, serve as contributing editor to the *Boston Weekly Magazine* and publish a collection of original songs, a volume of poetry and write three more novels. *Reuben and Rachel* appeared in 1798, *The Exemplary Wife* in 1813, and *Charlotte's Daughter*, found in manuscript at Mrs. Rowson's death in 1824, was published four years later.

None of Mrs. Rowson's other novels equaled *Charlotte Temple's* popularity. Over 160 editions appeared in the next hundred years and, until challenged by *The Wide, Wide World*, it was the over-all best seller in American fiction. However, despite the prejudice against novels, *Rebecca* attracted enough readers to justify six reprintings by 1831.

The latter novel followed the pattern set by Samuel Richardson's *Pamela*. *Rebecca*, the young heroine, whose "knowledge of mankind," said Mrs. Rowson, "was gleaned from a small though not ill-furnished circulating library," had apparently read and profited by Pamela's experience.

Both girls were befriended by a rich woman and, after her death, pursued by her son. Both resisted all blandishments until eventually their respective roués reformed and proposed marriage.

A little more novel reading might have saved Mrs. Rowson's Charlotte Temple from following so closely in the footsteps of another of Richardson's heroines, Clarissa Harlowe. At fifteen Charlotte was seduced by Montraville, a young officer, and under promise of marriage ran away from school in England and accompanied him to New York. Montraville, however, needed a rich wife and when he met a prospective candidate, a young lady with "a lively disposition, a humane heart and an unencumbered income of seven hundred a year," he readily believed reports of Charlotte's misbehavior made by a jealous rival and cast her off. Without friends or money, Charlotte bore their child in a hovel, lingering just long enough to die in the arms of her father who belatedly arrived to take her home.

In her preface to *Charlotte Temple*, the author claimed she had the story "from an old lady who had personally known Charlotte" and there is some reason to believe a relative of Mrs. Rowson's, Colonel John Montresor, actually was the original of Montraville.

Readers certainly found it extremely plausible, wept over Charlotte's unhappy lot and made pilgrimages to her supposed grave in Trinity Churchyard. Such things could and did happen all too frequently.

In proof, three years after *Charlotte Temple's* first American appearance, another popular novel, *The Coquette* by Mrs. Hannah Foster, told a similar tale and this, too, was "founded on fact," probably the seduction and suicide of Elizabeth Whitman, a young belle of Hartford, Connecticut.

Hannah Webster Foster, the author, born in Boston in 1759, was well connected, beautiful and clever. In her early twenties she began contributing political articles to a local newspaper. Among her many readers was John Foster, a clergyman, who sought an introduction and soon proposed. They were married in 1785 and twelve years later, after the birth of two daughters, Mrs. Foster wrote *The Coquette*. Mr. Foster was distantly related to Elizabeth Whitman and the details of her unfortunate story must have been thoroughly canvassed in the family.

As Mrs. Foster refurbished the scandal, Eliza Wharton (the alias which concealed Miss Whitman's identity) was young, gay and almost too independent. She rejected a suitable offer of marriage because she found the maker a pompous bore and liked another suitor, Major Sanford, better. The latter was so charming that even after Eliza found his intentions not strictly honorable she dallied on with him.

"To associate is to approve; to approve is to be betrayed," said Mrs. Foster, and so Eliza fared. For, like Charlotte Temple's Montraville, Major Sanford needed money and he soon found and married a handsome, agreeable girl "with five thousand pounds in possession and more in reversion" and left Eliza to die destitute and alone in childbirth.

Scores of lesser known heroines shared the same fate before the novel of seduction gradually went out of style. By 1801 readers could enjoy Tabitha Tenney's satire, *Female Quixotism,* and even laugh at her novel-reading Dorcas who changed her name to Dorcasina, romanticized every scoundrel she met and longed to elope in a chaise, declaring, ". . . it has been my supreme wish and expectation to realize the tender and delightful scenes so well described in these enchanting books."

There was one last fallen woman in the popular novel before the lists were closed, Mrs. P. D. Manvill's *Lucinda, the Mountain Mourner* in 1807. Lucinda ran away with Mr. Brown under a promise of marriage frequently repeated but never kept and eventually she, too, like all the others, came home to have her baby and expire in parental arms.

For death, at home or abroad, seemed the only possible solution under the circumstances. The ignorant and gullible, the stupid and silly, the clever and rebellious, it made no

31

difference—whoever broke the rules forfeited her life, not so much to an avenging God as to an implacable society that provided no respectable way to live on.

In her last days Lucinda read *Charlotte Temple*, deriving the doubtful consolation that it is better, comparatively at least, to die among friends than strangers. When heroines patterned themselves upon each other rather than upon life, the cycle was completed.

Although these novels, Richardson's *Clarissa* and *Pamela*, and many like them continued to attract readers well into the nineteenth century, no more fallen women appeared as popular heroines in American fiction for a century.

Several writers attempted serious studies—Rebecca Harding Davis' *Margaret Howth* in 1862 presented a realistic picture of a mill-town prostitute, in *We and Our Neighbors* in 1875 Harriet Beecher Stowe gave some attention to the problem of rehabilitating the wayward, but neither of these had large sales for no woman who bore the Scarlet Letter could win readers unless, like Nathaniel Hawthorne's Hester, she kept to the back streets of the distant past.

Prostitution did not cease; libertines and profligates remained at large; ladies sometimes loved unwisely but the fallen woman vanished from the novel of native origin.

In English and European fiction a frail creature might still stoop to folly, but not a popular American heroine. *She* had to be drugged, tricked, coerced, mesmerized, hypnotized or otherwise ensnared, for never of her own free will and knowledge would a trueborn daughter of the Republic accept a relationship outside of marriage.

Not virtue but economics wrought this new morality. In the earliest stages the Industrial Revolution in England depreciated marriage as an institution. When production left the home and one member of the family, usually the husband, followed the machine, he alone bore the whole burden of supporting several individuals. Consequently, early marriages offered few attractions; large families became liabilities and the position of women suffered.

Prudent men like Montraville and Sanford looked for a wife with money to pay for her keep and the girl without portion or prospects faced an uncertain future. The flights and fancies, the retreats and advances, the vaporings and affectations of the sentimental heroines through three, four, even eight volumes of attempted seduction concealed a very unsentimental struggle for existence.

In the New World, where the clock had turned back for a short historical moment to a pre-Industrial Revolution society, quite a different situation existed. With production in the home again, women and children became extremely valuable assets while on the frontier and the farm a family was a positive necessity. More than capital, social position or even education, labor made wealth in early America. Moreover, as customary in new settlements, a surplus of men (which persisted in some areas until the twentieth century) increased the bargaining power of women.

Virtue, more than its own reward, had come to be a valuable commodity in a rising market. There was a time when a Charlotte Temple, a Lucinda, an Eliza could be viewed sympathetically, but a later heroine who followed the same course—who threw away an asset for which bidders competed on every side was either subnormal or deranged, an object of clinical, not literary, concern. As a topic for fiction the wages of sin, worse than dishonor, came to be disinterest.

Feminine readers turned for a time to the Gothic novel made so popular by Monk Lewis, Mrs. Radcliffe and Horace Walpole. Chief among their many imitators in the United States was Isaac Mitchell. His *Alonzo and Melissa*, published first in 1811 and at least twenty times thereafter, went back to *Romeo and Juliet* for a plot although he added the proper quota of apparitions, robber bands and haunted castles and, as a concession to national optimism, carried the false burial to a happy conclusion.

These pretty horrors could not compete very long with the real, if less spectacular, ones in daily life. Women were ready for and found a new kind of reading—the domestic novel. These tales at first glance seemed full of the old sensibility and sentiment. Outwardly, little had changed. Marriage was still the primary goal of women, except now that they had become the sought rather than the seeker and they could, if they were clever, make better bargains. The conflict no longer arose from the woman's struggle to acquire a husband but rather from her efforts to control him and the marriage.

In 1794, Mrs. Rowson set the keynote for the next century and a half in her play *Slaves in Algiers*. She took the leading role and at the curtain's fall she came to the center of the stage and spoke the epilogue:

> " 'Well, Ladies, tell me—how d'ye like my play?
> 'The creature has some sense,' methinks you say;
> 'She says that we should have supreme dominion,
> And in good truth, we're all of her opinion;
> Women were born for universal sway,
> Men to adore, be silent and obey.' "

4 ❧ The New Reader

Between 1830 and 1850, 1,150 works of fiction by native authors were published in the United States—more than five times as many as in the preceding sixty years. This was a time of growth and prosperity, of energetic action and applied ingenuity, and literature, like everything else, flourished in the expansive climate of the period.

Optimism, almost synonymous with patriotism, assumed the quality of a virtue in the national character. Despite severe economic depressions in 1837 and 1841, Americans had faith in themselves and in their country—never before or since, perhaps, with such good reason. Foreign oppressors vanquished; political unity achieved; a model state established—these triumphs provided a gratifying past. To a people who possessed abundant land and natural resources, together with the experience and courage to use these gifts to the best advantage, the future seemed equally bright. Furthermore, the new democratic forces that brought Andrew Jackson to the Presidency in 1829 promised that all, through full male suffrage and its concomitant, free education, should have an equal chance to share in the rising fortune of their nation.

During the first half century of independence the dream of Jefferson, Paine, Freneau and others of a system of free schools, although accepted in theory, received, in actual practice, little support. While the Federalists and later the Whigs held power taxes went to protect property rather than to teach paupers. After Jackson's inauguration public schools increased and by 1840 the New England States, New York, Pennsylvania and Ohio all offered some degree of free education to their children without the stigma of charity and the movement spread—slowly throughout the South, rapidly in the West. A generation learned to read.

At the same time technical progress in this best of all possible worlds also stood ready to further art and disseminate culture while serving the body politic. Papermaking and binding methods improved and the introduction of the perfected cast plate by David Bruce in 1813 began a revolution in printing. Under the old system, using the hand-set type, frames had to be broken and reset as a book progressed, since few printers owned enough spare type to set an entire volume. Consequently, a first edition often proved a last. The new cast plates (the stereotype and, later, the electrotype) not only permitted more impressions and hence more copies than hand-set type but, as an added advantage, might be stored for later printings. By 1830 New York City alone had eight or nine stereotyping firms turning out a stream of Bibles, texts, hymnals and other standard works.

Among the many who contributed to the development of printing, the Hoe family deserves special mention. Robert, the father, began building presses in New York in 1805 and Richard, the son, introduced the first rotary press in 1846. The Hoe tie to the book trade was further strengthened by the marriage of Richard Hoe's sisters to Moses Dodd and Edward Mead. In the second generation, cousins founded

Dodd, Mead and Richard Hoe's daughter married J. Henry Harper, a partner in the publishing firm established by his grandfather.

Oil lamps, replacing candles almost everywhere, added several reading hours to the day. Better transportation—toll roads, new canals and later the railroads—permitted a wider distribution of books and periodicals than ever before. Crossroads stores stocked the latest poetry, gift annuals and novels; hawkers peddled biographies, Bibles and sermons through the backwoods. Subscription libraries trebled between 1825 and 1850. A number of enterprising young men, quick to scent the potential profits, set up as publishers and by the forties were flooding the market with cheap paperbacks that sold, in some cases, for as little as seven cents a copy. Wider education and the growth of the middle class had made the printed word a commodity suited for mass production and mass consumption.

The new reading public, although immeasurably larger, lacked the homogeneity of the old. Until the nineteenth century "literature" had been the concern of gentlemen. Chap books, ballad sheets, scurrilous pamphlets served the gutter trade but "books" were both written and read by a small, well-educated, predominantly masculine minority in the upper or upper-middle class who shared similar backgrounds, interests and ideals. The expanding, restless, complex society of nineteenth-century America no longer provided this single audience, but many. Although a Dickens, a Scott, or a Cooper sometimes possessed the alchemy to reunite readers for a little while, special groups with special needs soon discovered, perhaps created, writers who understood and reflected their

37

special, if unconscious, demands. Chief among the new customers to be pleased by publishers were women.

For girls took advantage of free education with even greater alacrity than their brothers although they braved strong opposition in doing so. The woman who could write, it was seriously argued, might forge her husband's name; the study of geography would encourage her to run away, and reading to neglect her home duties.

Despite these dangers, public schools offered a bargain in education few parents could resist. It cost the individual the same whatever the number or the sex of the children he sent to class so daughters went as well as sons and sometimes for more terms since a girl's service had less cash value than a boy's.

Coincidentally as women learned to read they also gained the leisure to practice their new accomplishment. The kitchen stove perfected between 1830 and 1850 made fireplace cookery, slow, dirty and laborious, happily obsolete; the increased use of cotton textiles and, after 1846, the sewing machine simplified another major task of women, clothing the family.

Further, the new prosperity at least along the Atlantic seaboard required the lady again. The swelling tide of immigration gave upper- and upper-middle-class women an opportunity to employ domestic help on a greater scale than ever before.

What did this growing feminine audience read? About the same books men did at first. The newly literate in both sexes, once they conquered the mystery of the printed page, demanded that it reflect and extend experience—disclose and resolve the contradictions of the outer and inner worlds—

clarify, inform and, most important, amuse. These tasks, traditionally performed by the folk tale, fiction now assumed.

From the beginning the English and European novelists enjoyed the widest distribution in America. Publishers preferred their books obviously since in the absence of an international copyright agreement, little or no royalty had to be paid on them. Native talent, faced with such competition, languished until an increasing multitude with a strong sense of nationalism demanded writers who could present the unique quality of American life and character. For readers, while delighting in the works of Scott, Dickens, Thackeray, and Bulwer-Lytton, also wanted tales with heroes and heroines cast in their own image, a climate and landscape they recognized, actions and incidents that proved the individual could solve his own problems and, subject only to heavenly ratification, control his own destiny in true democratic fashion.

James Fenimore Cooper and others met this need by adapting the historical novel for home use. Scores of stories of the Revolution, the frontier, of Indian attacks and captivities, of fur traders, scouts and minutemen re-created and glorified the past.

Nor was the contemporary scene at home neglected by writers or reader. Best sellers of the thirties included a slave memoir, two anti-Catholic exposés, a "true crime" novel, a political satire, four regional studies, a volume of homespun humor and several collections of sketches in which travel notes, local color and legends, philosophy, short stories, character impressions, and verse were combined in the half-fact, half-fiction form that Washington Irving did so well and his imitators so poorly.

39

There was also a growing literature *for* women *by* women. Reading, it seemed, incited writing. Scarcely an editor, but complained of being overwhelmed by visits, letters and manuscripts from "fair contributors" who seemed determined to push into the profession through every literary back door they could pry open or break down. Happily, the times favored their assault.

Not a few of the more ambitious tried their hand at the full-length novel and found publishers. Those who wanted to serve an apprenticeship on shorter pieces had a market in the new periodicals mushrooming everywhere. Sixty-four ladies' magazines alone began publication between 1830 and 1850— and although many failed, it cost so little, relatively, to start another that few interests, cults, reformers or regions lacked an organ to spread their particular gospel.

This was the heyday, too, of the Annuals—*The Friendship's Wreath, The Garland, Crown, Dew Drop, Pearl, Forget-Me-Not*—"elegant collections of choice selections suitable for each and every occasion be it birthday, holiday, wedding, birth or bereavement." They absorbed quantities of textual material to balance the steel engravings, lithographed illustrations, hand-colored presentation pages and inlaid, embossed, tooled bindings which really sold the volumes.

That women possessed a peculiar affinity for fiction was soon conceded and in not very complimentary terms, justified on the grounds that concocting untruths, disseminating gossip, prying into the affairs of others were an inherent part of the female character.

Beyond whatever truth this charge contained was the additional fact that writing, small and precarious though the returns might be, offered women a way to earn a living in one of the few professions men had not monopolized and fiction required the least formal knowledge or education to produce.

Thus when Mrs. Sarah Josepha Hale, left a widow at thirty-four, found she could not support her five children as a milliner, she tried literature. Her husband's Masonic brethren sponsored her first book, a collection of poems, and on the strength of this she devoted her whole time thereafter to her pen. Her first novel, *Northwood*, in 1827 attracted little immediate attention but a collection of her magazine pieces published two years later under the title *Sketches of American Character* went into eight editions by 1843.

Lydia Sigourney, who married a widower with three children and found his reputed fortune nonexistent, earned one of her own contributing to magazines and annuals. A compilation of her sketches in 1834 had six reprintings in the next ten years.

Less pinched by poverty perhaps, but nearly as prolific, was Miss Catharine Maria Sedgwick, sometimes called the first domestic novelist. While her earliest books, *A New England Tale* in 1822 and *Redwood* in 1824, did not rank among the best sellers of the decade, her audience increased with each new and similar novel she wrote.

"True fact" accounts still lured readers not quite ready to sink to outright romances. Mrs. Caroline Howard Gilman, the wife of a Unitarian minister, enjoyed considerable success with her *Recollections of a New England Bride* in 1834. When the author accompanied her husband to his new church in South Carolina she found material for a second volume, *Recollections of a Southern Matron,* "a novel based on fact—all but the love passages."

Mrs. Gilman attributed the thanks and congratulations she said she received from every quarter to the fact that her work "was the first attempt . . . to enter into the recesses of American homes and hearts . . . the first unveiling of what I may call the Altar of Lares in our cuisine."

Although each of these early novelists could claim some share in establishing the domestic novels form, none of them contributed to the eventual content, for their homely moral tales of everyday middle-class life, while admitting the frustrations and injustices women faced, offered no solution but submission and endurance.

In Mrs. Gilman's *Recollections of a Southern Matron* the heroine gave very specific instructions on how to make the best of married life when the honeymoon waned.

At first the heroine confessed:

I mused about past days; my views of life became slowly disorganized, my physical powers enfeebled; a nervous excitement followed; I nursed a moody discontent and ceased a while to reason clearly. Woe to me had I yielded to this irritable temperament. I began immediately on principal to busy myself about my household. . . . I was careful to consult my husband in those points which interested him without annoying him with mere trifles. If the reign of romance was really waning, I resolved not to chill his noble confidence but to make a steadier light rise on his affections. If he was absorbed in reading, I sat quietly waiting the pause when I should be rewarded by the communication of ripe ideas. If I saw that he prized a tree which interfered with my flowers I sacrificed my preference to more sacred feeling; if any habit of his annoyed me I spoke of it once or twice calmly and then bore it quietly if unreformed. I welcomed his friends with cordiality. . . . Stopped my yawns . . . This task of self-government was not easy. To repress a harsh answer, to confess a fault and to stop (right or wrong) in the midst of self-defence in gentle submission sometimes requires a struggle like life and death, but these *three* efforts are the golden threads with which domestic happiness is woven. . . . How clear is it then that woman loses by petulance and recrimination. Her first study must be self-control almost to hypocrisy. A good wife must smile amid a thousand perplexities and clear her voice to tones of cheerfulness when her frame is drooping with disease or else languish alone. . . . Let him know nothing of the struggle which follows the first chill of the affections; let no scenes of tears and apologies be acted to agitate him, until he becomes accustomed to agitation; thus shall the star of domestic peace arise in fixedness and beauty above them and shine down in gentle light on their lives. . . .

Women wrote four more best sellers before the decade ended, all of them on how to endure another of life's trials, one almost as difficult as marriage, poverty. For despite a general prosperity in the years following Jackson's election, the economic millennium had not arrived and 1837, in particular, was a time of bank and business failures, devaluated currency, vanished savings and deflated booms.

Miss Sedgwick's *A Poor Rich Man and a Rich Poor Man*, published that year, preached a gospel of militant optimism. Susan May, the heroine, the progenitor of Mrs. Wiggs and Pollyanna, showed how simple and satisfying it is to support a large family, dispense charity and educate children on meager wages, a pleasure denied those unfortunate enough to be wealthy. Miss Sedgwick had a social conscience. She supported the abolitionist cause; she worked among the poor;

she served on the board of the New York Prison Association; in *A Poor Rich Man* she noted the high rents slum dwellers paid for poor housing, but none the less she sincerely believed, "In all our widespread country there is very little necessary poverty. In New England none that is not the result of vice or disease."

In 1837, Mrs. Hannah F. S. Lee in *Three Experiments of Living,* frankly subtitled, "A Tract," warned her readers that marital happiness depended upon living within one's income, a proposition she demonstrated with Jane and Frank, a rather wooden pair who enjoyed domestic bliss in poverty but drifted apart when they spent as much and finally more than they earned.

Mrs. Lee, a widow with three children to support, understood the changing economic system slightly better than Miss Sedgwick and very sensibly pointed out that ladies who made fancy articles and sold them for charity deprived needy gentlewomen of their trade. She scolded women who made servants call again and again for wages due them and she pleaded for justice, not charity: ". . . pay . . . well and give . . . less, it would be better . . . for all."

With *Elinor Fulton,* a sequel to *Three Experiments,* a new style in feminine fiction began. Elinor, the twenty-year-old daughter of Jane and Frank, made feminine capital of her family's bankruptcy. Not content merely to save money and spread cheer, she fell to and supported the whole household, and contrived and planned and inspired and held the family together until her father recouped his fortune.

Mrs. E. L. C. Follen's *Sketches of Married Life* in 1838 had an equally competent heroine in Amy, who wanted to

44

teach an infant school but was discouraged by her well-to-do father on the grounds that such misplaced charity "only interferes with the wise designs of Providence." Poverty, he assured his daughter, would soon die out of itself but for the mistaken efforts of benevolent enthusiasts—a theory he was soon able to test, for he lost his own fortune.

Although Amy's privations were great—she had "to dress in factory cottons, give up a fire in her bedroom, her copy of Audubon, her domestics"—she rose to the occasion and she, too, supported the family and, if this were not enough, further defied society by going to the hospital and nursing her desperately ill fiancé back to health.

Neither *Elinor Fulton* nor *Sketches of Married Life* could compare in popularity in the decade of publication with *Three Experiments of Living*. Their world seemed not quite ready to accept these efficient young ladies. If sales are proof (20,000 copies in the first two months, twenty-one editions in nine years, and the further flattery of a parody, *Fourth Experiment of Living*, which sold almost as well), readers still preferred Jane, who squandered money, insulted old friends and relatives, toadied to snobs, drove her husband to ruin and then sat in the parlor and pitied herself.

Nevertheless, Elinor and Amy deserve a niche in the American heroines' Hall of Fame as the first of the indispensable women—the prototype of thousands who were to follow in their footsteps—the leaders of those gallant, resourceful, competent females who still occupy themselves in radio and television dramas, in short stories and novels—and in real life in rectifying some new masculine error.

5 ❦ The Scribbling Women

THE LADIES who created popular fiction in the thirties disappeared from the best-seller lists of the forties. Their earlier books continued to be reprinted but they did not repeat their success.

Free lancing proved almost as precarious as millinery for Mrs. Hale and she went to the *Ladies' Magazine* in Boston, where her work attracted the notice of Louis Godey who brought her to Philadelphia to edit his *Lady's Book* for forty years. Her influence upon her sex was great. She advocated better education and professional training for women; she set up workshops for sailors' wives and pleaded for sailors' libraries; she supported Howe's work with the blind; she made Thanksgiving a national holiday; she compiled biographies and contributed to the magazine she edited, but of her creative work nothing survives but her deathless verse, "Mary Had a Little Lamb."

Mrs. Sigourney confined her talent to short pieces (she specialized in the obituary poem) and became the largest single contributor to Annuals in the United States. Mrs. Follen wrote juveniles, teachers' manuals and poetry, translated Fénelon, served actively in the antislavery movement, edited a children's magazine, collected the works of her deceased husband in twenty-five volumes and tutored her son and other young men for entrance to Harvard University. Understandably, she found no time for any further excursions into fiction. Mrs. Lee, after a few more short novels, gave her whole attention to serious writing in the field of biography, history, art and criticism. Mrs. Gilman edited magazines and anthologies. Miss Sedgwick continued to turn out her domestic tales but none of the half dozen titles she published before she died in 1867 achieved the sales of *A Poor Rich Man and a Rich Poor Man.*

Almost the only work of fiction by an American woman to achieve any real popularity in the forties was *Alderbrook.* Its author, Miss Emily Chubbuck, in the tradition of her predecessors, wrote out of acute need—she longed for a new dress and hat in the latest style. Having money for neither, she sat down and "for very idleness without object or plan" wrote to Nathaniel P. Willis, the editor of the New York *Mirror,* and proposed he send her "a head-adorning, complexion-softening Neapolitan with a little gossamer veil dropping daintily on the shoulder of an exquisite balzarine." In return she offered him some stories. "I have plenty buzzing my head," she wrote, "and a pen—not a gold one, but a sturdy quill. I have Dr. Johnson's Dictionary, a good edition . . . and after I use up all the words in that I will supply myself with a Websters."

Willis, who built his own career on impudence, knew its market value and accepted the offer. The letters of Emily Chubbuck, renamed Fanny Forrester, became a regular feature of the *Mirror* and in 1846 Burgess and Paine published a collection of them as *Trippings in Authorland.*

Handicapped perhaps by this rather obscure title, the book attracted little notice until reissued shortly thereafter by Ticknor and Fields as *Alderbrook*. Then it sold so well that the publishers gave the young author a bonus and promised her double royalties on her next work.

Fanny Forrester was mawkish and lugubrious and as fond of deathbeds, orphans, falling tears and fading flowers as any of her readers. She accepted the mores of her time—she believed death or marrying one's employer provided the best escape from poverty; she declared a woman who utilized her talents in public would soon realize that "the eyes levelled upon her are a humiliation"; she thought victims of seduction and their offspring were happiest in the grave.

Nevertheless, flashes of wit and moments of satire illuminated *Alderbrook* and the young author glimpsed some of the realities her contemporaries ignored. In her novelette, *Grace Linden,* she presented a stark picture of an eight-year-old girl at work in a spinning mill.

Whether Fanny Forrester would ever have made a novelist —good or popular or perhaps even both—must remain forever a question. While *Alderbrook* was in press its author met a distinguished missionary home from Burma, the Reverend Adoniram Judson, twenty-nine years her senior, and widowed for the second time a few months earlier. They married and soon the bride saw the error of her former ways and apologized by inserting a dedication in her book:

To him who is henceforth to be my guide through life, its sunlight and its gloom, these few little flowers gathered by the wayside before we had met are half tremblingly but most affectionately dedicated. May their perfume be grateful, their fragility pardoned and heaven grant that no unsuspecting poison may be found lurking among their leaves.

As to a future course, the frontispiece showed the author herself, head raised, eyes toward heaven, hand over heart, declaring, "Henceforth to holier purposes I pledge myself."

The Judsons went off to Burma, where before long the Reverend Adoniram died. The young wife, left with an infant and several stepchildren to support, fell ill and like one of her own heroines came home with burning cheeks, glittering eyes and a racking cough. Working against time to earn enough to ensure the future of her children and her parents she wrote a biography of her husband and of her predecessors in his affections, missionary reports and Sunday-school tales. None of these appealed to the *Alderbrook* audience, and at thirty-seven Fanny Forrester, the merry girl who longed for the "stylish neopolitan . . . the exquisite balzarine," was dead.

During most of the forties popular fiction was controlled by two men, J. H. Ingraham and T. S. Arthur, who between them wrote 111, or almost 15 per cent, of the 765 novels which appeared.

Born the same year, 1809, the first of the pair to publish was J. H. Ingraham. His blood-and-thunder thrillers, full of cutthroats, rum bibers, pirates and prostitutes, sold as fast as he turned them out—in one year alone he wrote twenty novels and earned $3,000 thereby he boasted to Longfellow whose pen brought him $517 in 1842.

Ingraham, after his marriage to Miss Mary Brooks, the cousin of Phillips Brooks the hymnologist, gave up his lurid tales and became an Episcopalian minister. In 1855 he wrote a Biblical novel, *The Prince of the House of David*, which brought him a small fortune. At his wife's suggestion he used a portion of this untainted wealth to buy up and destroy the progeny of his youthful imagination.

Timothy Shay Arthur, almost as prolific with fifty novels between 1842 and 1850, was a wiser man and sought from the very first to please the ladies. Born in Newburgh, New York, Arthur, at six, moved with his parents to Baltimore, where almost at once the series of misfortunes that led him to literature began.

After a few months in school the teacher pronounced young Arthur too stupid to learn and advised his father to remove him. Apprenticed to a watchmaker, it took the boy seven years to learn a trade usually acquired in half that time and then, before he had an opportunity to use his hard-won knowledge, his eyesight failed. Arthur, by then in his early twenties, went west as an agent but before long his employers were bankrupt. Arthur came back to Baltimore and in a last desperate effort to survive joined a friend and "took on a literary paper."

"I have never had literary ambition. I am a literary man through force of circumstances," Arthur apologized to his anonymous (and only) biographer, adding, "I have tried hard to make my way in life in pursuits outside literature, but every effort to do so has proved a failure and a loss and I have been driven back to my pen work again and again."

Although his first magazine venture proved unprofitable, Arthur found work on local papers and betweentimes free-lanced, turning out a steady stream of stories, sketches, poetry, articles and juveniles.

In 1837, Louis Godey, a rarity among editors of the period because he paid cash for contributions to his *Lady's Book,* accepted a manuscript from Arthur, sent him $15 and a request for more domestic tales.

Arthur, delighted, complied and three years and several hundred thousand words of finished copy later he had mastered the art of producing that ever-salable item, the formula story. Despite his lack of confidence in his business ability he proved equally skillful at marketing his wares. He moved to Philadelphia "to be close to the good magazines." As soon as he finished his first novel he wrote Appleton's suggesting they might use it in their newly inaugurated series, Tales of the People and Their Children, but before sending the letter he took it to his good bookseller friends, Robert and John Hart, and asked for their endorsement. Robert Hart was glad to tell Appleton's that he knew T. S. Arthur and believed his book would be sure to sell. Below this, John Hart slyly added that his brother, Robert, wanted to send the manuscript to the Harpers "at this moment when they are running a series of native stories against you but . . . Appletons should do something of the same kind and no one in the country is better qualified than Mr. Arthur."

Appleton's succumbed to this sales pressure and published Arthur's *Tired of Housekeeping* in 1842.

Arthur's style was simple and lively; he had a good ear for colloquial speech and even Edgar Allan Poe conceded that "Mr. Arthur is not without a rich talent for descriptions of scenes in low life but is uneducated and too fond of mere vulgarities to please a refined taste."

There was some truth in Poe's criticism. In his very earliest stories Arthur rivaled Ingraham in gore and violence but like any good businessman he sought to please his clients. Once Arthur discovered what Mr. Godey and his subscribers liked and paid for he did his best to deserve their valued patronage. Arthur's lack of education and taste were, if anything, advantages that enabled him to meet his readers on terms of equality.

In many ways his tales resembled the anecdotal, self-help articles of the present day. Taking a timely, mildly controversial social problem—boarding out, runaway marriages, feminine extravagance in dress, mothers-in-law, preoccupied husbands, unruly children, Arthur would build a story comprehensible to even the most inexperienced reader. He presented the subject quickly; he used simple homely incidents and one-dimensional characters; he arrived at an acceptable solution without wasting time or words. If a young lady full of false pride snubbed a seamstress on page four, by page twenty-four she had lost her own fortune and suffered the same treatment and by page thirty-four had reacquired wealth and new humility.

Arthur preached, moralized and dispensed platitudes but he also offered his readers some sound advice and he honestly tried to show how some difficult problems in social adjustment might be solved with common sense, mutual compromise, calm discussion, intelligent planning and a more liberal education.

He had for his time some remarkably advanced ideas. Perhaps remembering his own unhappy youth when, as he said, "I needed careful patient judicious training I couldn't get," he insisted children could be taught more through kindness than with strict discipline. Neither was he, by his own

52

admission "a regular Sunday religionist . . . who saw sin in pink ribbon and carnal mindedness in a blue bonnet." The hard work of life, he suggested, ought to be balanced by fun and pleasure, even dancing, and he dared to add, "one person can commit more sin going to church than another to the ballroom."

His real sympathy for the victims of many social injustices of his day won him, at least for a time, the title of "the Dickens of America." In a series of sketches he illustrated the trials of immigrant girls, bound servants, domestics, apprentices, seamstresses, and urged their women employers to accord these exploited creatures more understanding and sympathy, better working conditions and prompter pay.

He probably chose intemperance as a theme for his second novel in 1842 because it was a lively social issue. Intemperance had always been something of a problem in the New World where distilling seemed the only way to solve the equation of long distances plus available raw materials plus hazardous transportation plus time. But when the molasses turned into rum and the grains into whisky, replacing the milder beverages, the ales, beers and wines of Europe, appetite and habit remained the same. The yearly increase in the consumption of distilled spirits, far in excess proportionately to population growth, caused grave concern to many.

Almost from their founding the Society of Friends and the Methodists had worked for temperance and soon the Congregational Church joined the crusade. In 1808 the first temperance society was formed in Moreau, Saratoga County, New York. In 1825, Lyman Beecher, the father of Harriet Beecher Stowe, preached six rousing sermons, later published and widely circulated, on the subject. The following year the American Temperance Society was organized and by 1836 claimed almost eight thousand local groups with a combined membership of a million and a half.

The temperance movement, from the first, contained several factions. In the minority were those who actually advocated "temperance," or moderation, but did not completely condemn the use of alcohol; others permitted wine and beer but frowned on spirits; most militant of all were the T Totalers, so called because their pledge cards bore a conspicuous T for Total Abstainer.

Schisms developed over questions of method and procedure. Could the drunkard best be saved through legislation, prayer, strong coffee, increased revenue taxes, reading rooms, cold water baths or (predating Alcoholics Anonymous by a century) self-help. To the last-named one group of temperance workers, the Washingtonians, ardently subscribed and it was their true story Arthur reported in his second book and first great success, *Six Nights With the Washingtonians*, published in 1842.

The movement began when six confirmed drunkards met in a bar and, as Arthur recounted it:

Something they felt in the presence of each other made them hesitate to order. Soon the feelings of each other became known to the others and they felt a sudden hope spring up in their minds, a hope in the power of association. Sad experience had proved to each one of them that alone he could not stand. But together, shoulder to shoulder . . . heart to heart, that though the struggle would be hard, they could conquer.

Like their modern counterpart, Alcoholics Anonymous, the Washingtonians believed that only an alcoholic could really understand and consequently help an alcoholic. So, while other workers in the field besieged legislatures and castigated rum sellers, the Washingtonians waited at saloon doors, urging all who would listen to join them and meet weekly for mutual encouragement and aid.

"These meetings," said Arthur, "are very interesting as they relate their experiences, they are touching, simple, unadorned histories of real life told by participants, though sometimes they are humorous and amusing" (a sentiment visitors to the testimonial meetings of Alcoholics Anonymous often echo).

For four years, aided in some degree, no doubt, by Arthur's book, the Washingtonians triumphed. They sent out missionary teams whose arrival in a town usually meant a general holiday, a parade, a mass meeting addressed by public officials and new converts by the hundreds, sometimes the thousands.

Unfortunately, the very elements which should have ensured real success for their movement brought about its downfall. Other temperance groups, alienated by the Washingtonians' disinterest in legislative action and in the religious and spiritual aspects of the problem, withdrew their support and co-operation. The Washingtonians might have survived this had not stronger and more subtle opposition come from an unexpected quarter.

The temperance movement launched by men remained until mid-century under their direct control. In 1852 Susan B. Anthony attended the convention of the Sons of Temperance as a delegate from the ladies' auxiliary, the Daughters' Union. Being refused the floor on the grounds that "sisters were not invited there to speak but to listen and learn," she left the hall followed by several sympathizers. With the help of Samuel P. Townsend, a manufacturer of sarsaparilla, the women's own temperance movement began and despite desertions, splits and masculine maneuvering grew in power and prestige.

For the Washingtonians the alcoholic himself was the center of interest. When women entered the picture, however, the focus of attention shifted to the secondary victims, the family and associates of the drunkard, and to the plight of his mother and sister, his wife and children, all sympathy and concern were thereafter directed as if in some obscure way the alcoholic might be cured by dramatizing those who suffered at his hands.

No longer was there any therapy in one alcoholic helping another in a meeting of equals. A few semireformed characters like J. B. Gough, the lecturer, attained prominence in the movement but proffered aid came to be more and more authoritarian. From a moral pinnacle the employer, the clergyman, the temperance "speaker," and especially the long-suffering wife and the innocent child pleaded with a lost, degraded inferior and, all too often, pleaded in vain.

T. S. Arthur understood and accepted this new conception. In his next temperance book (and his greatest success), *Ten Nights in a Barroom,* in 1854, the drunkard himself is almost ignored, reduced to a token prize in the real struggle between a pair of heroines, his wife and daughter, and a villain, the rum seller.

Arthur was one of the few novelists of the period who understood that a serious sex struggle was in progress. He tried to define its cause and to offer a real solution for the increasing marital discord he observed on every side.

He was no feminist. A *bad* marriage, he pointed out in *Married and Single,* is better than *no* marriage. *Fanny Dale,* published the same year, 1843, illustrated his belief that in any real difference of opinion it is the wife that must yield. But he took husbands sternly to task in dozens of tales for their insensitivity, their absorption in business; he urged men to devote more time and money and interest to their families, to be helpful, courteous and understanding at home, to express their appreciation and affection frequently and to share their cultural interests and recreations with their domestic partner and allow her some chance for education and independent action. Successful marriages, Arthur pointed out again and again, require the admission of faults, good-humored tolerance and mutual sacrifice on both sides.

The philosophy of compromise made little appeal to women. The days of any yielding, of any submission were over. Arthur's feminine audience did not want *their* faults discussed, *their* behavior corrected. Equality might have satisfied that vociferous minority agitating far and wide for women's rights but the quiet, sweetly smiling ladies at home sought, though perhaps unconsciously, another goal—complete domination.

Arthur, with his acute appreciation for the nuances of social change and his knack for making literary capital of it, dramatized this issue in his novel, *What Can Women Do?* (1856) by contrasting two families, the Penroses and the

Eldredges. In the former the "right" kind of feminine influence prevailed but in the latter Mrs. Eldredge summarized her philosophy:

Men are pretty hard subjects in the main but a resolute woman is, nine cases in ten, a match for the hardest. We have a stronger self-will and more endurance and therefore we can hold out longer. Men, after a certain period of opposition, grow weary but a woman's spirits never tire, do you understand that?"

"I think," replied her neighbor, "your meaning is clear."

For Arthur's feminine audience it was, if anything, almost too clear. Arthur found himself deserted for a new school of domestic novelists, all women, who veiled any such calculating aims and techniques under misty clouds of pious sentiment, fragile innocence, artless gaity and heroic martyrdom.

Arthur, astute as always, soon realized this and tempered his frankness, changed his style, tried the longer novel, gave more attention to plot and to character development, even, as early as 1847, donned wig and crinoline and prefaced his *Young Lady at Home* with ". . . in writing this book the author in order to make it both useful and interesting has assumed the character of an American woman and caused her to relate her own experiences."

Ingraham, too, tried a similar disguise. Shortly before his death in 1860 from a self-inflicted gunshot wound, he signed his last novel, *The Sunny South,* with the nom de plume Kate Conyngham.

It was not enough. A successful writer for women, more than a journalist or storyteller or instructor or reformer, had to be a high priestess in a growing cult.

Among the earliest who assumed this office was Mrs. E. D.

E. N. Southworth. For readers nourished on short tales, sketches, homiletic parables, she provided more sophisticated fare in the form of a full-length novel, *Retribution*. It was, despite a hundred faults, a remarkable work for a novice.

The author appeared in the wings and bungled on and off stage like a careless scene shifter. A useless subplot, that might better have been saved for another book, told the story of the beautiful daughter petted and adored until her father's death revealed she had the fatal drop of Negro blood that condemned her to the auction block and a life of shame, a theme other writers borrowed again and again for the next fifty years.

Yet, stripped of the "elegant prose," "refined dialogue" and some of the melodramatic incidents, the author showed a deep psychological understanding of the interaction of character in this story of Hester Grey, an orphaned heiress who grew up in a boarding school. Plain, shy, serious and lonely, the girl's intensity repelled her schoolmates and made her the victim of the first opportunist who came her way, Juliette, "a beautiful, fascinating but selfish unprincipled girl to whom the plain simple-hearted and generous heiress furnished a most convenient and easy dupe."

Hester, called home to her estate, fell in love with her guardian, Colonel Dent, the son of a brilliant father, his senior by less than twenty years. Only in constant competition could the younger man find the reassurance, the sense of entity he needed. In his political career "he could live through furious storms of opposition; the dangerous dead calm of neglect but was in danger of being wrecked on the shore of success." When he saw that Hester adored him, he introduced a rival and under this stimulus was able to propose to her because, as he said, "If I do not secure you someone else may come along and snatch you away and that idea I cannot contemplate with kindness."

Hester's abject devotion amused, bored and finally irritated Colonel Dent and when, shortly after her marriage, Hester invited Juliette to live with them, the end was inevitable. Here the author's understanding of character, of the play of personalities upon each other, showed to excellent advantage and her observations, in view of modern psychological knowledge, were profound. She perceived that not only do oppressors make victims but in some deeper and more subtle way victims make oppressors.

Colonel Dent and Juliette fell in love. Hester never realized the situation and her stubborn innocence intensified their guilt, and when at last she died loving and trusting them both, the pair were truly doomed—with all hope of absolution finally gone.

Juliette and Colonel Dent married but, racked by mutual mistrust, quarreled and then in the complicity of evil drew together again, time after time, until as last both were destroyed.

Mrs. Southworth, unlike many of her contemporaries, did not rely on the easy power and long arm of Divine Justice to resolve her plot. Her statement at the beginning of *Retribution* might have served as a symbolic brief in the case of women vs. men:

There are intangible crimes carrying in themselves the seeds of their own most bitter punishment—the punishment being nothing apart from or opposed to this sin, but simply the evil principle itself, in its final stage of development. In these instances no law may be able to touch the guilty—no upbraidings of conscience torment him—no visible judgement of heaven fall upon him—yet as surely as the plant is produced from the seed will the punishment be evolved from the sin. . . .

Published by Harper's and advertised as a work of major importance, *Retribution* had considerable success. While a few critics objected to any retribution not divinely administered, most reviews were enthusiastic. John Greenleaf Whittier in the *National Era* declared that few native novelists could surpass Mrs. Southworth. Her *Retribution*, in his opinion, was as good as, perhaps even better than, *Jane Eyre*. He found many to agree with him. Most propitiously a career that was to last half a century had begun.

Mrs. Southworth was but one of the many new writers. All through the countryside the scratch of pen on paper filled the air, and the century, reaching the halfway mark, found the women who would dominate fiction for the next fifty years hard at work.

Two Cincinnati matrons, Mrs. Caroline Lee Hentz and Mrs. Harriet Beecher Stowe, the former with a play and a novel, the latter with a textbook and a collection of short sketches already in print, were well on their way to successful careers. So, also, was Mrs. Ann Stephens of Maine, editor at twenty-two of a pair of magazines and author of several short stories and poems including the schoolroom recitation classic, "The Polish Boy."

Dozens of others still served their apprenticeships. Miss Mary Hawes, a Virginia belle of sixteen and a contributor of short stories to *Godey's* under the nom de plume Marion

Harland, put the finishing touches on her first novel, *Alone.*
Up in Massachusetts another, although unrelated, Miss Mary
Hawes, better known later as Mrs. Mary J. Holmes, at fifteen
was interrupting a teaching career begun at thirteen to write
and publish *her* first short story. Out in Texas seventeen-year-
old Miss Augusta Evans worked diligently on her father's
Christmas present—not the embroidered watch case nor the
pair of slippers most young ladies attempted but a novel,
Inez, A Tale of the Alamo. Most precocious of all, perhaps,
was little Isabella Macdonald—or Pansy, as she was known to
friends and neighbors in Rochester, New York. Her first story
appeared in the local paper shortly after she celebrated her
tenth birthday.

Susan Warner, isolated on her island home in the Hudson,
little suspected how much company—and competition—she
had as she worked on the manuscript of *The Wide, Wide
World.*

6 ❧ The Death
of the Master

CINCINNATI in the second quarter of the nineteenth century, with twenty-seven artists, seven sculptors, a library association, three colleges, three theological seminaries, schools of law and medicine, two musical societies, twenty-nine periodicals and an Academy of Natural Sciences, claimed, and with some justification, the proud title "Athens of the West."

The informal center of this cultural life was a club, the Semi-Colons, founded and presided over by Dr. Daniel Drake. Among the members who "met around" to recite poetry, read original contributions, declaim extemporaneously on suggested subjects and perhaps dance a Virginia reel after the refreshments were Mrs. Sarah King, later to found the Philadelphia School of Design, Judge James Hall, then editor of the *Western Monthly Magazine*, Salmon P. Chase, who became Lincoln's Secretary of the Treasury, Nathaniel Guilford, one of the most vigorous advocates of free schools, Christopher Cranch, Unitarian minister turned artist and poet, and two literary ladies.

The elder of this pair by eleven years was Mrs. Caroline Lee Hentz, the mother of five children and the wife of Nicholas Marcellus Hentz with whom she conducted a fashionable boarding school for young ladies in the city. Mrs. Hentz had begun her writing career most auspiciously in 1831 by winning $500 and a gold medal for a play, *DeLara or the Moorish Bride,* performed in both Philadelphia and Boston, she wrote short stories for the *Western Monthly,* and her first novel, *Lovell's Folly,* had just been published.

The younger of the two women in the Semi-Colon Club had also contributed to magazines and she, too, had won a literary prize, fifty dollars, for *A New England Sketch.* In 1843 Harper's published this and other short pieces by her in one volume, *The Mayflower.* The forties abounded in floral titles: Annuals, Collections, Periodicals bloomed on every side as *The Wreath, The Garland, The Moss Rose, The Lily* and *The Forget-Me-Not.* In addition to being fashionably botanical, however, *The Mayflower's* title indicated something of its content—tales of New England life and character. But, while the author caught the wry turn of the Yankee character and expression and the stark beauty of the northern scene, there was little to indicate that her next book would be the greatest selling novel of all time, *Uncle Tom's Cabin.*

The young author, as Miss Hattie Beecher, had accompanied her father, the Reverend Lyman Beecher, to Cincinnati from Connecticut when he assumed the presidency of Lane Theological Seminary late in 1832. The next year Dr. Calvin E. Stowe joined the faculty as Professor of Languages and Biblical Literature and his young wife, Eliza, and Harriet became intimate friends. When Eliza Stowe died in 1834 a common grief drew Harriet and the bereft widower together and in 1836 they married.

Calvin Stowe, a scholar fluent in nine languages and an

acknowledge authority on pedagogical methods and Sacred Literature, was nervous, pessimistic and something of a hypochondriac. Given to morbid fancies, he thought the spirits visited him and plucked his guitar strings to announce their presence. Fat, balding, ten years older than his bride, he did not present a very romantic figure, but he was a man—with enough confidence in his own masculinity, enough generosity and intelligence to be happy with a famous wife.

In temperament and personality Calvin Stowe's second wife was his direct opposite. All the Beechers were dynamic, vigorous, often violent, crusaders. Early in his career in the ministry, the Reverend Lyman Beecher, disgusted at the amount of drunkenness common at ordinations, preached a series of sermons which did much to bring about the later reforms. Harriet's older sister, Catharine, in addition to establishing schools for girls, published texts on sociology, theology, morals and housekeeping. Seven brothers, the most famous of them Henry Ward Beecher, were ministers of the gospel. Harriet Beecher, no exception to the family rule, possessed that combination of independence, ability, zeal, endurance, inspiration and inner conviction found so often in the New England character.

Although Mrs. Stowe's background and talents were exceptional, the pattern of her days in her early married life was commonplace in the extreme. Married at twenty-five, she bore seven children and buried one of them before her fortieth birthday. Like many women of her generation she was threatened with tuberculosis; she was often ill; she was usually tired. She managed on a small and irregular income and with the help of one servant did all the cooking, washing, cleaning, sewing, and baking for her family; sometimes she taught school and kept boarders; always she wrote. In a letter to her sister-in-law from Brunswick in 1850 she described her busy life shortly after Calvin Stowe accepted the Collins Professorship of Natural and Revealed Religion at Bowdoin College in Brunswick, Maine:

By day it has been hurry, hurry, hurry and drive, drive, drive! or else the calm of the sick room ever since last Spring . . . from the time that I left Cincinnati with my children to come forth to a country that I knew not of almost to the present time it has seemed to me as if I could scarcely breathe I was so pressed with care . . . a constant toil and hurry in buying my furniture and equipments and then landing in Brunswick in the midst of a drizzly inexorable northeast storm and beginning the work of getting in order a deserted, dreary old house. All day long running from one thing to another . . .

Then comes a letter from my husband, saying he is sick abed, and all but dead; don't ever expect to see his family again; wants to know how I shall manage, in case I am left a widow; knows we shall get in debt and never get out; wonders at my courage; thinks I am very sanguine; warns me to be prudent, as there won't be much to live on in case of his death, etc., etc., etc. I read the letter and poke it into the stove and proceed. . . .

Though in the last month of her pregnancy, Mrs. Stowe managed to have a sink made, the cistern barrels put into the cellar, finish "two sofas or lounges, a barrel chair, divers bedspreads, pillow cases, pillows, bolsters, mattresses, paint two rooms, revarnish furniture—what didn't we do?" before her husband arrived from Cincinnati and her son, Charley, was born. She continued her letter:

I was really glad for an excuse to lie in bed for I was full tired I can assure you. . . . During this time I have employed my leisure hours in making up my engagements with newspaper editors. I have written more than anybody, or I myself, would have thought. I have taught an hour a day in our school, and I have read two hours every evening to the children. The children study English history in school, and I am reading Scott's historic novels in their order . . . yet I am constantly pursued and haunted by the idea that I don't do anything. . . . Since I began this note I have been called off at least a dozen times; once for the fish-man, to buy a codfish; once to see a man who had brought me some barrels of apples, once to see a bookman; then to Mrs. Upham, to see about a drawing I promised to make for her; then to nurse the baby; then into the kitchen to make a chowder for dinner . . . and now I am at it again, for nothing but deadly determination enables me ever to write; it is rowing against wind and tide.

Another woman, one with equal talent but less stamina, might have succumbed to the physical and mental pressures and vented her frustration on those about her, but Mrs. Stowe, conscious of her failures, her ineptitude, her disinterest in many household duties, struggled on and somehow in the New England phrase "she managed" as she later wrote Mrs. Follen:

When a new carpet or mattress was going to be needed or when at the close of the year it began to be evident that my family accounts, like poor Dora's, "wouldn't add up" then I used to say to my faithful friend and factotum, Anna, who shared all my joys and sorrows, "now, if you will keep the babies and attend to the things in the house for one day, I'll write a piece and then we shall be out of the scrape."

The money was not the only motivating factor. Like all the Beechers, she was a crusader and deeply concerned with social reform. In her earliest sketches she pleaded for temperance, higher wages for seamstresses, better education for women. During her years in Cincinnati, though not then an abolitionist, she worked to help the Negroes, both free and fugitive, flocking across the Ohio from Kentucky. She told the story of one of these slaves in a short piece published in 1845.

Shortly after her arrival at Bowdoin her sister-in-law, Mrs. Edward Beecher, urged her to do more on this subject, saying, "Hattie, if I could use the pen as you can, I would write something to make this whole nation feel what an accursed thing slavery is."

Mrs. Stowe followed with interest the debate then raging in Congress over the proposed Fugitive Slave Act and with many other antislavery sympathizers deeply resented the support given the act by Daniel Webster's speech earlier in the year.

Reading her sister-in-law's letter aloud to her family, she promised them and herself, "I will write something. I will, if I live."

Little Charley, whose arrival in the summer had afforded his mother a needed vacation in childbed, had not, of course, been weaned. "As long as the baby sleeps with me nights," Mrs. Stowe wrote to her sister-in-law, "I can't do much at anything, but I will do it at last."

She kept her promise, and early in January, 1851, she began *Uncle Tom's Cabin*. "The thing may extend through three or four numbers," she wrote when offering the story to Dr. Gamaliel Bailey, the editor of the *National Era*. She had contributed to his antislavery paper before but she feared he might refuse this latest work, for the New Year's issue announced a serial by her friend, Mrs. E. D. E. N. Southworth. Dr. Bailey accepted, offering $300 for the story, and the first installment appeared in June. The "three or four" numbers grew to forty before Mrs. Stowe finished her task.

Meantime, on her sister's behalf Catharine Beecher offered Phillips and Sampson the book rights. They declined. The risk of losing money if it failed—or Southern customers if it succeeded—was too great.

Among the thousands following the fortunes of Uncle Tom, Little Eva and Topsy in the *Era* was Mrs. John P. Jewett, the wife of a Boston publisher, and at her insistence her husband agreed to take the book. He, too, thought the subject would prove unpopular and he told the Stowes they could either share the printing costs and profits with him equally or take a straight 10 per cent royalty. Professor Stowe chose the latter, and his wife hoped that perhaps from the proceeds, "I may have a silk dress."

By the end of the first month she realized her wish—an edition of ten thousand copies sold out, in the next four weeks forty thousand more, and the year's end saw nearly a quarter of a million copies in print, thirty editions in the British Isles alone and translations into both French and German. A dozen theaters in the United States and England were presenting unauthorized dramatic versions, there were Uncle Tom songs, pictures, poems, even an Uncle Tom and Little Eva game played with pawns.

In the one hundred years since *Uncle Tom's Cabin* first shook the soul of the world, critics have never tired of exposing the book's faults or of demonstrating again and again that

Mrs. Stowe violated every rule of literary construction, good taste and common sense in its creation. Readers, happily, had a different opinion and the total sale of *Uncle Tom's Cabin* remains unequaled by any other novel in any language.

If the book suffered from anything, it was this very popularity. As the story passed from literature to folklore, Mrs. Stowe's sound craftsmanship and creative artistry grew blurred and distorted and were finally almost obliterated. Her characters were no longer human beings, complex and contradictory, but only crude symbols of good and evil reduced to the simplest form. The constant repetition of the material in *Uncle Tom's Cabin* in abridgments, plays, juvenile versions, and the flood of imitations that followed made incidents, strong and fresh and vivid when Mrs. Stowe first used them, seem repetitious and stylized. Most to blame perhaps were the "Tom Shows," with a vapid, flaxen-wigged Eva, an acrobatic Eliza, a comic Topsy and the integrity and strength and purpose of Uncle Tom so distorted that his very name came to imply the sycophant and the hypocrite.

Readers who came to this great book with minds untouched by the later distortions are to be envied. For *Uncle Tom's Cabin* was and is a major work of art. The subject had freshness and originality. A few books like Mrs. Southworth's *Retribution* touched on "the fate of the beautiful quadroon" but less than a dozen dared any fuller treatment. Authors, no less than publishers, remembered the lucrative Southern market and ignored the issue.

Mrs. Stowe had a wealth of material to draw from—the slave market, the forced separation of families, the escape and pursuit of slaves, the contrast of plantation life in the cabin and the mansion, the exotic flora and brilliant landscape of the South, the peculiar sex mores, the extramarital activities, the whole folklore of miscegenation provided suspense, mystery, passion, color and dramatic action by figures of heroic stature. She exercised discrimination, caution and tact but she could be almost unbearably realistic. She was not afraid to show violence, brutality, lust, fear, corruption, although she did so with economy and restraint.

She realized what many did not—slavery destroys the master as well as the slave. Simon Legree no less than Uncle Tom was a victim. If an Eliza could dash across the ice to save her child, a Mr. St. Clare might not be so fortunate. His daughter, little Eva, died not from imaginary vapors but from witnessing horrors and cruelty she could neither endure nor change. Uncle Tom suffered physical pain; in St. Clare, Mrs. Stowe drew a moving portrait of a man in mental anguish, one who saw and hated the social evils of his world but, lacking courage to attack them, lived on guilt-ridden.

Uncle Tom's Cabin appeared at a propitious moment in history. Eighteen fifty-two was an election year. The passage of the Fugitive Slave Law, surprisingly, some thought traitorously, supported by Daniel Webster in 1850 and the divergent opinion regarding local enforcement of this act made slavery the main issue in a violent presidential campaign.

The book had a psychic timeliness as well. Mrs. Stowe's appeal could transcend the barriers of sex, class, religion, nationality, age, because it confirmed a decision already taken, if still unspoken, by most of the literate world. Moved by love or fear, by economics or history, by charity or justice, by sentiment or experience, men as individuals and in groups had finally rejected the institution of human slavery. Mrs. Stowe articulated that resolution.

During the novel's serialization the original sub title, "The Man That Was a Thing," was replaced by the more inclusive "Life Among the Lowly." Not only Negroes longed for freedom—English mill hands, German farmers, Norwegian fishermen, French seamstresses—men, women and children everywhere wanted their economic liberty—their just place in the world.

Despite the power and realism in *Uncle Tom's Cabin*, it was a domestic novel and a sentimental one as well. For, although Mrs. Stowe knew very well what slavery meant, the methods she suggested for abolishing the evil were hopelessly impractical, if not economically impossible. She and a number of statesmen and a large segment of the total population shared the delusion that manumission, gradual emancipation, Christian example, model plantations, colonization in Liberia, prayer or the workings of individual conscience would eventually solve the problem to the satisfaction of all concerned.

"This book is essentially domestic and of the family," George Sand said in reviewing the French translation, "with its long discussions, its minute details, its portraits carefully studied. Mothers of families, young girls, little children, servants even, can read and understand them and men themselves, even the most superior, cannot disdain them."

Nor did they, but the pages had an especial message for that large section of the "lowly," women. Women composed Mrs. Stowe's earlier audience and for them she described the slave coffles, the separation of families, the double servitude imposed upon women in bondage. It was to them she had old

Prue speak. "A man kept me to breed chil'en for market, and sold 'em as fast as they got big enough; last of all, he sold me to a speculator." Women would sympathize with Susan, remembering with a deadly sickness at her heart how the slave dealer had looked at her daughter, "lifted up her curly hair and pronounced her a first-rate article."

Mrs. Stowe knew she would touch feminine hearts with Mrs. Shelby forced to see Eliza her friend, confidant, almost sister, but still a slave, sacrificed to pay Mr. Shelby's debts. In the story of Eliza, herself, by the bedside of her baby son sold to a trader all mothers understood why: "No tear dropped over that pillow; in such straits as these the heart has no tears to give—it drops only blood, bleeding itself away in silence."

Only a woman could forgive Cassie, who passed from man to man, saw her first two children sold by their own fathers, and resolved her third baby should escape.

"Oh, that child—how I loved it! . . . But I had made up my mind—Yes, I had. I would never again let a child live to grow up! I took the little fellow in my arms, when he was two weeks old, and kissed him, and cried over him; and then I gave him laudanum, and held him close to my bosom, while he slept to death. . . . I am not sorry, to this day; he, at least, is out of pain. What better than death could I give him, poor child!

Although Uncle Tom, the nominal hero of the book, was male, it was not too difficult for feminine readers to identify themselves with him, too. He had the virtues—meekness, piety, humility, endurance—commonly assigned to women in exchange for independence. Moreover, although custom and sentiment gave women some advantages over the Negro, they occupied an unfortunately similar status before the law—so

73

much so that antislavery and women's rights were joint goals in many societies. The first Woman's Rights Convention at Seneca Falls grew out of the refusal of the World Anti-Slavery Convention in London in 1840 to seat eight women delegates from the United States. In this country, thereafter and with increasing frequency, the two reforms came to be combined in societies, periodicals, and the public mind. Wendell Phillips, spokesman for the abolitionists, promised "first the Negro then the woman."

Women responded to Mrs. Stowe from all over the world —George Sand from France, Jenny Lind and Frederika Bremer from Sweden, Anna Leonowens on behalf of a Siamese court lady, impelled to free all her slaves. Queen Victoria's friend, the Duchess of Sutherland, Lady Byron, Mrs. Browning and a half million other women in Europe and the British Isles filled twenty-six folio volumes with their greetings and signatures—and protests against slavery—and forwarded this Affectionate and Christian Address to Mrs. Stowe.

Uncle Tom's Cabin certainly converted some women to the abolitionist cause and won their support for the Civil War and for the various philanthropic and educational projects subsequently organized to help the newly emancipated. Whether it brought any recruits into the active struggle for women's rights is doubtful, but it did strengthen the revolt of woman no less than of serf or slave by sounding the death knell of the master.

7   The Mutilation of the Male

IN THE writing of *Uncle Tom's Cabin*, Mrs. Stowe had exhibited many of those qualities considered by her contemporaries to be sex-linked to females—sympathy, tact, sensitivity, sensibility. She mitigated the horrors of slavery with just masters, self-sacrificing mistresses, and noble Southerners; she made Simon Legree, the brutal monster who killed Uncle Tom, a New Englander born and bred. Abolitionists, she thought, might criticize her book. She willingly accepted that risk, for to conciliate, to influence, to persuade the South was her avowed mission.

She rejoiced when a woman "with strongly southern family ties" wrote: "Your book is going to be the great pacificator; it will unite both north and south."

So for a very short time it seemed.

Then the counterattack began. The South rushed to answer, ostensibly Mrs. Stowe, although the vehemence of their protests suggested a guilty conscience as their chief accuser. Apologists, each according to his own gift, sounded forth. Ministers preached sermons showing that Uncle Tom's Christian character resulted directly from the missionary opportunities slavery provided. Politicians drew up statistics proving free mill hands in New England fared no better than Negroes in the South, a sentiment with which Mrs. Stowe heartily agreed. A number of Southern gentlemen, forgetting their vaunted chivalry, stooped to personal attacks upon Mrs. Stowe and her family.

In the North abolitionists, churchmen, merchants, manufacturers, friends and admirers of Mrs. Stowe rallied to her support, defending themselves and their own institutions in the process.

Novelists, of course, both North and South, made the controversy particularly their own. In the decade after *Uncle Tom's Cabin* appeared, a half dozen writers explored the same theme. Fresh material could still be found to illustrate the antislavery argument, and although every page bore testimony to a growing abolitionist sentiment, the authors occasionally allowed some virtues to exist below the Mason-Dixon line and even a few faults above it. Dwarfed by Uncle Tom most of these novels with their authors were soon forgotten.

The opposition meantime, as though awaiting a signal, had also burst into print. Some of the "answers" to Mrs. Stowe were hastily assembled magazine pieces, such as Peterson's *Life in the South,* or reissues of earlier books. Sarah Josepha Hale's *Northwood,* first published in 1827, was reprinted in 1852 and the following year she took time from her editorial duties on *Godey's Lady's Book* to write *Liberia,* another novel with the same theme. In both books Mrs. Hale condoned slavery on the grounds that Negroes lacked education for freedom, and proposed gradual manumission and emigration to Africa in some distant future as the best solution to the vexing question. Fifteen other original works of fiction with a justification of slavery did appear between the publication of *Uncle Tom's Cabin* and the outbreak of the Civil War—nearly half of them written by women.

It would be hard to know what women born and bred close to slavery could find defensible in the institution. It gave the rich white woman a servant to pick up her handkerchief and open her fan; it ensured the poor white woman her chastity, or so she was told. As a matter of unromantic fact, the mistress of a large plantation had heavier and less easily delegated responsibilities than her husband. She was burdened with the lifetime care, training and supervision of an unwilling, and consequently not very efficient, corps of workers, a task that Southern women, all observers agreed, usually carried out with energy, kindness and devotion. Paradoxically, the poor white woman in the South who needed work was barred from earning a living at manual employment customarily reserved for slaves. Most important of all—as long as white men had free access to Negro women the position and health and bargaining power of white women suffered.

The South was full of literary ladies articulate, not to say garrulous, on a variety of subjects. They patriotically supported the culture, cuisine and climate of their native region and with the changing times, state's right, secession and the Confederacy. But when it came to defending slavery as an institution, the native-born and -bred Southern women kept discreetly quiet and let those with less firsthand knowledge, less real experience answer Mrs. Stowe.

Most popular among the dozens who rushed to do so was Mrs. Caroline Lee Hentz, Mrs. Stowe's old Cincinnati acquaintance and fellow member of the Semi-Colons.

The Hentzes and the Stowes were alike in many ways, so

77

alike perhaps that, although the limited society of Cincinnati in the 1830's threw them together frequently, they never became sufficiently intimate to continue their early friendship through correspondence or visits in later life.

Nicholas Marcellus Hentz, like Dr. Stowe, was an able scholar. The son of a French émigré, he spoke three languages, had received some medical training at Harvard College and displayed considerable talent in miniature painting, etching and engraving. Before his marriage to Caroline Lee Whiting in 1824 he taught with George Bancroft, the historian, at Round Hill, the school for boys in Northampton, Massachusetts. In the field of letters Professor Hentz had to his credit a classical French reader, a historical novel, *Tadeuskund, the Last King of the Lenapes,* and some curious, strangely modern short stories on interplanetary communication. Two of them, *Another World and This* and *Travels on a Ray of Light,* might qualify as the earliest examples of American science fiction. Although Professor Hentz earned his livelihood by conducting a series of boarding schools for young women, his real profession was entomology and his work as a collector, classifier, and illustrator received recognition from scientific societies here and abroad and his *Spiders of the United States* is still regarded as a definitive contribution in the field of arachnology.

Like Dr. Stowe, Professor Hentz had something of the absent-minded professor about him. He was given to unorthodox beliefs and mild eccentricities, to sudden and silent prayers with his head against any convenient wall. His friend, Oliver Wendell Holmes, supposedly modeled Scarabee in *The Poet at the Breakfast Table* upon him:

... As singular-looking a human being as I remember seeing out-side of a regular museum or tent show . . . round shoulders stooping over some minute labor . . . very slender limbs, with bends like a grasshopper . . . looks as if he might straighten them out all of sudden and jump instead of walking . . . voice a dry creak as if made by some piece of mechanism that wanted oil-ing. . . .

Both Dr. Stowe and Professor Hentz were quiet, retiring, inclined to ill-health, easily depressed, with a tendency toward melancholia, happier with ideas than with people. Both had the misfortune to live in an age that glorified the man of action and made much of the merchant prince, the planter, the sea captain, the scout, any who could turn opportunity into profit, but rewarded the scholar with little in payment or prestige. Both men—perhaps it was inevitable—had found for a wife their exact opposite.

Mrs. Hentz and Mrs. Stowe were talented, ambitious, rest-less, vigorous and eager to participate in the world. As novelists they needed people and life—and also leisure to practice their profession. If these husbands suffered from the temper of the times, so, too, did the wives. For they were doubly handi-capped by being women, and unusually gifted women, in a man's world.

In another society, one with less rigid patterns of masculine and feminine behavior, some exchange or modification of their sex roles might have permitted couples like the Hentzes and the Stowes more personal freedom and greater opportunities to utilize their separate talents. The nineteenth century did not. Good sense and good fortune enabled the Stowes to weather their matrimonial difficulties and work out a mutually satisfactory relationship that endured as long as they lived. The Hentzes were not so successful.

Like Mrs. Stowe, Mrs. Hentz had a New England background. Her father, John Whiting, after service in the American Revolutionary Army, settled in Lancaster, Massachusetts, where Caroline Lee was born in 1800 and lived until her marriage in 1824. Her first view of the South came in 1825 when she accompanied her husband to his post at the new College of North Carolina at Chapel Hill. After four years there the Hentzes moved to Covington and started a girls' school. The two years in Kentucky were followed by two in Cincinnati, nine in Florence, Alabama, two in Tuscaloosa, three in Tuskegee, four in Columbus, Georgia, and the remaining years in Florida, where they died within the same year, 1856, in Marianna and St. Andrews, little towns not too far, by coincidence, from Mandarin, where the Stowes spent the winters in their later life.

In five of the cities where the Hentzes lived they opened schools for girls; none achieved permanent success. Schools and teachers were luxuries growing communities eagerly sought but could not always support when they had achieved them—as the Hentzes found to their sorrow; nor did the scientific ability of Professor Hentz and the creative talent of his wife adapt to the routine drudgery of "finishing" young belles.

Neither of the pair was a good administrator. Mrs. Hentz's diary records their struggles: one day she must answer an ungentlemanly note from the uncle of a pupil, on the next she is forced to write a woman who has been repeating idle and unjust gossip, now a girl has left in anger, another is deceitful, three more are caught selling their clothes for eggs and sugar and fishes—each day brought a new problem.

Mrs. Hentz liked her pupils and they loved her. She could jump rope and play prisoner's base with them, arrange fetes and holidays, plan the coronation of a May Queen and preside over the commencement exercises, but she hated teaching.

During their stay in Florence, Alabama, Mrs. Hentz wrote in her diary: "Teachers are at the mercy of unreasonable and unprincipled children and credulous and prejudiced parents. You need the patience of Job, the wisdom of Solomon, the meekness of Moses and the adaptive powers of St. Paul to be sufficient for the duties of our profession."

Her pen might have released Mrs. Hentz from this drudgery, given her an opportunity for self-expression and an assured income, if she had possessed the time and energy and determination and freedom to do more than short bits— sketches, tales and verse. But besides caring for her four children, she managed the school farm and household, provided food, lodging, washing, nursing for thirty or more boarding pupils, helped teach a hundred day students, and aided her husband in collecting, classifying and arranging insects.

Through her contributions to Annuals and to the *Saturday Courier, Godey's,* the *Saturday Evening Post, McMahans,* the *Southern Literary Messenger,* Mrs. Hentz had acquired an audience. Strangers wrote to her and newspapers carried "some flattering remarks" on her work. In 1846 a collection of these magazine pieces, under the title *Aunt Patty's Scrap Bag,* sold well enough to encourage a publisher to issue *The Mob Cap,* which had won a $200 prize from the Philadelphia *Courier.* But not until Professor Hentz's declining health necessitated closing the Tuskegee school, the last they attempted, and the couple moved to Columbus, Georgia, could Mrs. Hentz devote her full time to literary work. Not long after their arrival she wrote her friend, Mrs. Stafford:

There is Dr. Wildman, our physician and Friend, so kind, so attentive, so very agreeable, intelligent and fine looking. He is a host in himself—He has shown an interest in my welfare for which I cannot be sufficiently grateful. It was he who strenuously urged me to give up my school and follow the vocation for which God endowed me. He said, "he would stand by me" and not to fear any consequences. He comes and I read to him chapter by chapter as I write and he animates me by his praise. You know that we much more frequently find a female friend, combining the qualities we admire than a male but when we do meet one of these rare jewels we ought to prize them.

Mrs. Hentz, in her earliest work, *Lovell's Folly*, in 1833, touched briefly on the problem of slavery, admitting that while many hard masters did exist "the evil is too deeply rooted to be extirpated at once."

In her next full-length novel seventeen years later she gave the subject even less attention. *Linda; or, The Young Pilot of the Belle Creole* had a plantation setting and slaves, sometimes comic, sometimes pathetic but always deft, were like the wood fires, ever-blooming gardens and bountiful tables, part of the furnishings. *Rena; or, The Snow Bird*, published the following year, had an indeterminate locale and not a single reference to Negroes in any capacity.

Mrs. Hentz's first real defense of slavery came in that crucial year, 1852, in her novel *Marcus Warland*, the story of a poor boy and his sister, befriended by Mr. Bellamy, a rich plantation owner, who educated the children and reformed their father, a drunken ferryman, by making him an overseer of his slaves. These latter Mr. Bellamy could not free lest he expose them to want and temptation. So he gave them gardens, had a dancing pavilion built for their entertainment, and provided beautifully frosted cakes "white as ivory," oranges and confections for their weddings. The grateful recipients of these favors understandably refused any opportunity to change their lot, and the author concluded:

It is true they were slaves but their chains never clanked. Each separate link was kept moist and bright with the oil of kindness.

Marcus Warland was probably in press before Mrs. Hentz saw *Uncle Tom's Cabin.* Her direct answer to Mrs. Stowe came two years later in *The Planter's Northern Bride.*

This story opened as the editor of an abolitionist newspaper, the *Emancipator,* brought a fugitive slave home to occupy the best bedroom, eat at the table and associate with his family, including his lovely daughter, Eulalia. At the same time Russell Moreland, a rich, young, handsome Southern planter, arrived in the village and met Eulalia. Her father's misplaced charity to runaway slaves had kept the family poor but Eulalia fortunately possessed the foresight to protect her hands with thick woolen mittens while dusting, sweeping and sewing and consequently "justified the admiration of the fastidiously observing Moreland," who proposed. But Eulalia's father forbade her marriage to a slave holder although Moreland argued:

I look on every master and mistress in our southern land as a missionary appointed to civilize and Christianize. Give me your daughter and look upon her . . . as the wife of a Christian missionary.

So Moreland waited, befriending meantime a "northern slave," an ill and destitute woman cast off by her employers. Before long Eulalia took cold, went into a decline and soon appeared

the faint meandering blue veins . . . visible through her alabaster skin . . . the long pensive eyelashes and the eyes languishing brightness . . . all signs of the fatal beauty which marks the victim of consumption . . .

Her father relented and the happy couple, joined in matrimony, departed for Moreland's plantation. There, surrounded by "wealth and luxury . . . a tea service of the most delicate porcelain . . . massy, glittering silver . . . a horse black and shining as ebony . . . a beautiful white pointer spotted with bright bistre . . . negroes in close attention," two nurses for each child and more slaves who refused freedom, Eulalia lost her abolitionist sentiments. So, too, did her father, for immediately he paid her a visit he admitted that

. . . if all masters establish as excellent regimes and enforced them with the same kindness, wisdom and decision, the spirit of abolitionism would die away for want of fuels to feed its flame.

Conversion by visitation, far from original with Mrs. Hentz, had been used in at least three novels before *The Planter's Northern Bride* and so frequently thereafter that the whole body of proslavery fiction sometimes seemed one great travel folder to entice the North on a mass excursion trip below the Mason-Dixon line.

Mrs. Hentz's reasons for writing the book were numerous and complex. She said she wanted to heal the breach she saw widening on a visit, the only one she ever made, to her old home in Massachusetts in 1853. Perhaps she also had an old score to settle with Mrs. Stowe. The preface declared that

our National honor is tarnished when a portion of our country is held up to public disgrace and foreign insult by those, too, whom every feeling of patriotism should lead to defend it . . .

Mrs. Hentz was also astute enough to know that a timely subject helped sales. Early in 1854 she wrote her publisher:

Having so long looked in daily expectation of hearing from you and been disappointed I thought I would write and learn why my book delayed its appearance. Everyone says the excitement produced by the Nebraska Bill will be favorable to its reception.

Whether Mrs. Hentz had any real personal concern about slavery is doubtful. In her first contact with Negroes she displayed the ambivalence customary to most newcomers to the South. From Portsmouth en route to North Carolina she wrote her sisters:

You see such a swarm of greasy negroes filling the houses and streets. It is enough to put one out of conceit with everything.

But once established at Chapel Hill she discovered an embryonic poet in George Moses Horton, a Negro fruit peddler, who with her assistance and patronage wrote and published several poems including a funeral ode for the Hentzes' first child, a two-year-old son, who met an accidental death shortly after the family reached the college.

The Hentzes owned no slaves and Mrs. Hentz's understanding of Negroes never increased—indeed, her books testify she neither saw nor heard them.

In *Lovell's Folly* she offered as Negro dialect:

"Me no care about water sparkles. Me getting homesick. I 'fraid hav't seen no chance of bacon and greens since come here—folks no know what good here."

Without recognizing even the simplest of stylized gambits slaves employed to appease the vanity of their masters, she reported "as the very description a negress gave of herself in our own family in comparing the negro race with the white":

"Look a' me, black as de chimney back—dey white as snow. What great big thick ugly lips I got—deres look just like roses. Den dis black sheep head—dey got putey soft long hair just like de silk ribbons."

Yet Mrs. Hentz fully comprehended the Negro's real function in the South. In her diary she noted:

met a bride—she is not handsome, not even pretty nor witty but her father owns four or five hundred negroes and that makes her lovely in this southern land.

Therein lay the key to Mrs. Hentz's defense of slavery, to the real tragedy of her life, to her continued appeal to an audience. For Mrs. Hentz *was* handsome, more than pretty, and *very* witty, but she lacked the proper qualifications to make her lovely in the Southern land.

"Conspicuous both in person and manner was Mrs. Hentz whom none saw without admiring," so Edward Mansfield of

Cincinnati described her in 1832, "she was what the world calls charming."

Mrs. N. H. Olmstead, a guest in the same house with Mrs. Hentz in Columbus, Georgia, almost twenty years later remembered her "as a little above medium height . . . every motion graceful and full of gentle dignity . . . her arm could have been a sculptor's model . . . she had deep violet eyes, a Grecian nose, a firm sweet mouth with character and emotion in every line . . . she was an elegant and accomplished woman whose presence had an indefinable charm never to be forgotten and she was observed and admired by all."

Yet what had her beauty and grace, her talent and intelligence brought Mrs. Hentz? Nothing. No money, no settled home, no acknowledged position—only work she hated attended by humiliations she never learned to endure. She had lived for twenty-five years on the edge of the plantation aristocracy—allowed to watch but never to possess its careless luxury, graceful ease and unconcerned security.

Her short stories "The Pet Beauty," "Ugly Effie," "The Two Sisters," "Mary Hawthorne" and a score of others were Cinderella tales, with the rich and proud brought low and the simple, good and deserving elevated to their places.

As much as the monetary reward for her work, Mrs. Hentz wanted the prestige, the acceptance it would bring. "Should no northern heart respond to our appeal," she wrote in the preface to *The Planter's Northern Bride*, "we trust the voice of the south will answer own own."

The grateful citizens of Columbus did present Mrs. Hentz with a purse of $200, a piece of jewelry and named a generation of girls in her honor, but the South could not support its

87

native talent as even the great William Gilmore Simms discovered. Once the whole region had been an important book market where subscription agents and traveling book peddlers found a hospitable welcome for themselves and their wares in the great houses, and newspapers announced with equal fanfare the arrival of the newest Scott from England and the latest bonnets from Paris. Slowly, almost imperceptibly at first, the hopeless struggle to make slave labor return the same profit as free labor took its toll. In 1790 the population and the wealth of the North and South were approximately equal. Seventy years later, at the outbreak of the Civil War, the North possessed three-quarters of the national wealth in mines, manufacturing, transportation, and two-thirds of the total population.

In the North and West the middle class increased rapidly and public schools and libraries were making readers the new technology demanded. In the South, meantime, the pattern was reversed as more and more good plantation acreage, slaves and capital were concentrated in the hands of fewer and fewer people.

Some of the dispossessed moved west to Arkansas, Texas, eventually to California in search of free land or new occupations. Others retreated into a proud and hopeless aloofness and in Crackers, Wool Hats, and Hillbillies the accident of illiteracy became a chronic affliction. In the earlier plantation days the benign mistress or well-disposed young people in a family sometimes taught their house servants to write their names and read the Bible, but the statutes of many states and communities soon forbade this charity on the grounds that a literate Negro might "get ideas."

The Northern mechanic with a shelf of "well selected titles" the pioneer pushing west, his books stored under the wagon seat, by force of numbers became more important book buyers than the Southern planter who gave a carte blanche order for "any choice works suitable for a gentleman's library or lady's work table."

Fortunately for Mrs. Hentz, the real appeal of her books did not lie in their propaganda content. Indeed, she sold as well or better in the North, and a generation after Emancipation the Boston Public Library counted her among the three most popular authors on their shelves.

Her novels had little plot, less suspense and no humor, but her keen sensory perception and her natural facility of expression gave her work the "exquisite color" and "charming style" her generation admired. She possessed an undeniable talent for self-dramatization that imparted a certain life and intimacy to her pages. For her the novel was an open letter to the world wherein she presented, explained and justified herself and bestowed compliments and criticism on her associates.

The libelous content of her first novel, *Lovell's Folly,* supposedly caused its withdrawal. In *The Planter's Northern Bride* she portrayed Cincinnati society and paid her friend, Dr. Drake, "an imperfect tribute to his exalted worth, brilliant and commanding talents and pure and genuine philanthropy," and perhaps she was still thinking of the Stowes when in the same book she introduced an abolitionist couple, both canting hypocrites, named Softly who dressed with "Quaker-like precision and neatness" and lured contented slaves from loving masters.

All the Happy Endings

Her deepest grievance, the one she continually tried to resolve in her novels, was with life itself. How could she or any eager, intense, curious woman like her find a way to use her talent and beauty and charm to any real advantage without violating convention. To remain unmarried was unthinkable. The few legal benefits spinsters enjoyed scarcely balanced the restrictions custom imposed on their dress, movement and behavior. Without inherited wealth, their economic status was most precarious. The very skilled and aggressive might enter, at half a man's wages, one of a few trades or professions. The New England mills offered almost the only industrial employment and women of education and ability and intelligence responded so eagerly to this opportunity that the mill girls of Lowell, Massachusetts, with their reading clubs, dramatic societies and chorus groups became famous. The equalitarian tradition precluded household service as a profession and in any event the influx of immigrants after 1835 offered keen competition in this field. In Protestant America few convents offered a refuge. Even missionaries, it was often pointed out, must be married to endure the trials or perhaps the temptations of life among the heathen. The majority of single women lived on, at best as tolerated dependents, at worst as unpaid drudges in a relative's household.

Like all whose economic and social position is insecure, the old maid was an object of ridicule and in the domestic novel, at least in those written by married women, a figure of humorous scorn—the traditional butt of jokes. Mrs. Hentz herself drew several of these sharp, bitter, ill-formed, ill-tempered eccentrics.

Yet marriage imposed almost equally severe restrictions,

for the ambitious wife had little chance to demonstrate her wisdom, her courage, her value—as long as a husband fortified by legal and social authority dominated the relationship. But if in some way the power of the male could be diminished or removed, then neither conscience nor society would censure the brave woman forced to act on her own initiative.

Few whole men appeared in Mrs. Hentz's novels. In *Linda* the heroine's father was almost an imbecile; her tutor and her stepbrother, who both aspired to her hand, were moral cripples, violent, untrustworthy and jealous. When Linda did marry, her husband obligingly died at sea. Heroines found it easier to love a man if, like Marcus Warland, he was stricken with fever. Even then a possible recovery always threatened.

In *Eoline* that young lady promised St. Leon on his deathbed that she would marry him. Soon "every line was glowing with the inspiration of returning health . . . but she felt no answering enthusiasm. . . . St. Leon, blooming in health and radiant in hope was a very different being to her from St. Leon languishing on a sick and dying bed."

Most autobiographical of all Mrs. Hentz's novels was her last, *Ernest Linwood,* subtitled to remove any doubt, "The Inner Life of the Author."

Mrs. Hentz had long persuaded herself, her children, many of her friends and finally her readers that her husband's morbid suspicions and violent jealousy had darkened their entire married life and shattered their happiness. In *Ernest Linwood* she told a story, thinly disguised, of their sojourn in Cincinnati, where a Colonel King, a distant relative of the Beechers, madly enamored with her charms addressed an improper letter to her. Instead of returning it, she at-

tempted an answer, was detected by her husband, who be-
haved like a maniac, and only the intercession of Dr. Drake
and the immediate removal of the Hentzes to Florence, Alabama, prevented a duel and bloodshed. The story, or at least
some of the details, was probably true. Although why the
Hentzes rather than Colonel King left town, along with some
other puzzling features of the story, remains a mystery.

Ernest Linwood's wife, gentle, blameless Gabriella, of
course, did nothing to arouse his suspicions. Nevertheless, his
attacks of jealousy grew so frequent and frenzied that in a
moment of penance he vowed to lock himself in the library
for forty days. He bade Gabriella adieu:

Would to God I had never crossed your path or roses with my
withering footsteps! Would to God I had never linked your
young, confiding heart to mine, so blasted by suspicion, so con-
sumed by jealousy's baleful fires! Yet, Heaven knows I meant to
make you happy. I meant to watch over you as tenderly as the
mother over her new-born infant—as holily as the devotee over
the shrine of the saint he adores. How faithless I have been to
his guardianship of love, you know too well. I have been a mad-
man, a monster—you know I have—worthy of eternal detestation.

Gabriella answered:

"Farewell, Ernest," said I, slowly retreating, "may angels
minister to you and bear up your spirit on their wings of love!"
I looked back, on the threshold, and met his glance then
turned toward me. Had I been one of the angels I invoked, it
could not have been more adoring.

It is doubtful if Mrs. Hentz was any more a Gabriella than
her husband was an Ernest Linwood, although her diary for
the period immediately after she left Cincinnati might have

borne for its subtitle "The Inner Life of a Sentimental Heroine." For on one day she was Folly Repentant and on another Innocence Accused and after that Virtue Vindicated. She played in turn the Coquette, the Belle, the Femme Fatale, the Injured Wife, the Erring Heart. A bluebird could set her philosophizing and so could a flag carried by the troops going to Florida to fight the Indians; if she saw the moon "it looks precisely like one of Ossian's moons"; and when the fire went out it was not only cold but "oh, how the vision of the past dim and awful floated around me as I sat by the fading embers in the loneliness of the midnight hour. That past, I fear which will ever more give its color to the future."

She palpitated at the prospect of a visit from Dr. Drake—whether she did so out of joy, sorrow, fear, guilt, boredom or the sheer pleasure of palpitation would be hard to determine.

She inquired darkly, "Must we carry to the altar of duty our purified and still burning affections and meet there but cold approval and toleration? Yes, all is unavailing but Heaven still guides the path of the erring and I dared to hope resentment would die over the coldness and darkness of the tomb."

Meantime, Professor Hentz, singularly unaware of his somber reserve and volcanic outbursts, fenced the garden, tended his silkworms and completed, labeled and packed his great insect collection which he had sold to the Boston Museum for $500. He bought his wife a pair of vases with "Remember Me" on them, a few days later he gave her a silver pencil and, whenever he could find an hour to spare, persuaded her to go fishing with him.

Professor Hentz never received quite the recognition his contribution to science justified—nor the rewards his talents deserved. Perhaps, too, life in the shadow of a brilliant, accomplished, attractive wife intensified certain insecurities, self doubts he possessed. Certainly as the years passed, Professor Hentz grew more and more to resemble the creature of his wife's imagination until finally he became what his eldest son, a physician, called "a miserable hypochondriac—unfit for work."

In 1854 the Hentzes left Columbus for Florida. Professor Hentz went to their married daughter in St. Andrews. Mrs. Hentz stayed with her son in Marianna and worked to support them both, going back and forth to nurse her husband through his worst relapses. She wrote to her friend, Mrs. Stafford:

Another thing I will say to you frankly, just as I would speak if I were sitting by your side, in that dear chamber of yours and holding your hand in mine, that restless feeling which you know, prevented Mr. H. enjoying my *male* friends, seems to have subsided during his illness. He seems so distressed on my account that the support of the family has fallen on me that he rejoices in anything that contributes to my happiness from whatever source it flows. So heaven in kindness modifies our trials. He is exceedingly patient, gentle, and grateful—reads a great deal and paints when he feels well enough. He takes Laudanum and morphine constantly—a dreadful necessity.

Those women who were not fortunate enough to get a bad husband had to make one.

8   Keepers of the Keys
to the Kingdom

To MAIM the male, to deprive him of the privilege
of slavery and the pleasure of alcohol was not, of course,
enough. Female superiority at the same time had to be established and maintained. Beginning with Mrs. Follen's
Sketches of Married Life and Mrs. Lee's *Elinor Fulton*,
writers of the domestic novel seized every possible opportunity
to demonstrate the marked ability of women in the practical
concerns of everyday life—not a difficult task, for often a self-
portrait sufficed. Several had achieved real success, a recognized name and an assured income. A few earned what for the
times represented solid fortunes. One semiannual royalty
payment alone brought Susan Warner $4,500 although this,
like all her money, went to support her family and pay off
her father's old debts—which unfortunately encouraged him
to contract new ones.

While *The Wide, Wide World* was still in press, Susan
Warner began her second book, *Queechy*, published by Putnam in April, 1852, had the largest advance sale in the firm's
history, 5,000 copies.

"The Wide, Wide World," said the *North American Review*, "struck a chord that was still vibrating when Queechy

came along to prolong the thrill. . . ." Elizabeth Barrett Browning wrote to her friend Miss Mitford, "Tell me if you have read Queechy? I think it very clever and characteristic. Mrs. Beecher Stowe scarcely exceeds it after all her trumpets."

English, French, German and Swedish editions followed and, like *The Wide, Wide World*, *Queechy*'s title passed from literature into the language. The book's locale, thinly disguised, soon became identified with the countryside around Canaan, New York, where Susan Warner often visited at her grandfather's farm. Tourists, eager to see landmarks and acquire souvenirs, arrived there in parties. Residents obligingly changed the name of their Whiting Pond to Queechy Lake and a local industry turned out Queechy rifles. A British packet in the Australia trade was christened *The Fleda*, after the novel's heroine, and a neighbor of the Warners echoed the compliment by naming his rowboat *The Queechy*.

It was not strange that readers who liked Susan Warner's first book accepted her second with almost equal enthusiasm, for with slight variations in plot, incident and character they told the same story.

Fleda Ringgan, like Ellen Montgomery, was an orphaned girl left in the care of relatives. She, too, wept and sang hymns and read her Bible and was befriended by a handsome, rich, gallant Englishman whom she later married—but there were two notable differences between these heroines. Ellen Montgomery seemed scarcely able to perform the simplest duties. Timid, unassertive, nervous, she could do little but read and memorize prodigious numbers of facts. She burnt the chocolate, tangled her sewing and demonstrated little skill and less interest in the routine tasks of everyday life.

But Fleda was drawn to another pattern. A true spiritual descendant of Elinor Fulton and of Amy in *Sketches of Married Life,* she could and did manage her own affairs and those of her friends and relatives. She raised vegetables, made bread, cobbled shoes, boiled maple sugar, sold flowers, and in her uncle's absence managed his farm so profitably she converted the neighborhood to a whole new method of agriculture.

But to excel in practical matters only was not enough for women—spiritual concerns, too, now came within their orbit. In The Wide, Wide World Ellen received religious training and direction as tradition decreed from wise, learned, devout men, the son and brother of her friend, Miss Alice.

In *Queechy,* the roles were reversed and twelve-year-old Fleda assumed the moral leadership when Mr. Carleton, twice her age, asked:

"How do you know there is a God? What reason have you for thinking so out of the Bible?"

It was a strange look little Fleda gave him. He felt it at the time, and he never forgot it. Such a look of reproach, sorrow and pity, he afterward thought, as an angel's face might have worn. The question did not seem to occupy her a moment. After this answering look she suddenly pointed to the sinking sun and said, "Who made that, Mr. Carleton?"

Mr. Carleton's eyes, following the direction of hers, met the long bright rays whose still witness-bearing was almost too powerful to be borne. The sun was just dipping majestically into the sea, and its self-assertion seemed to him at that instant hardly stronger than its vindication of its Author.

A slight arrow may find the joint in the armor before which

many weightier shafts have fallen powerless. Mr. Carleton was an unbeliever no more from that time.

Women showed their eagerness to perfect themselves in this promising new part by their enthusiastic reception the next year, 1854, of two novels, *The Lamplighter,* by Maria Cummins, and *Alone,* by Marion Harland, the pen name of Mary Virginia Hawes.

Miss Cummins, the elder by three years, was born in Salem, Massachusetts, in 1827. Her father, a judge, supervised her early education and fostered her precocious talent and later sent her to the famous girls' school at Lenox, kept by Mrs. Sedgwick, the sister-in-law of the novelist, Catharine Sedgwick, who often visited the establishment. Inspired, perhaps encouraged, by the august presence of the author of *Redwood, A Poor Rich Man* and so many other domestic tales, Maria Cummins, after her graduation, began contributing to the *Atlantic Monthly.*

Her first novel, *The Lamplighter,* published by J. P. Jewett and Company of Boston, who did so well with *Uncle Tom's Cabin,* won immediate acceptance—40,000 copies sold in the first eight weeks, 70,000 before the year ended. An English edition and several foreign translations further extended the audience. In Philadelphia, T. B. Peterson, whose dexterity in jumping aboard any passing literary bandwagon was proverbial, advertised *The Watchman* by an anonymous author "as a fitting companion piece to The Lamplighter."

Marion Harland, too, had a devoted father who encouraged her to write. Born in Amelia County, Virginia, educated first at home and later at one of the "old field schools" peculiar to the region, she spent her early life in and around Richmond with frequent visits to nearby plantations. At fourteen she began contributing to a local journal and by the time she was sixteen her first short story in *Godey's*, "Marrying Through Prudential Motives," had been pirated in turn from an English magazine, across to France, back to England and from that source repirated home again.

Maria Cummins spent the latter part of her life in Dorchester, Massachusetts, and Marion Harland occasionally visited her father's family there—for Mr. Hawes, like many Southerners, was a transplanted New Englander. The two authors once met and in her autobiography Marion Harland described the encounter:

> In 1855 no other woman writer was as prominently before the every home and gossip of the personality of the author was seized upon greedily by the press and readers. She was to take tea at the house of my cousin, Francis Pierce. I was sitting by the window of the drawing room awaiting her arrival and gazing at the panorama of Boston Bay and the intervening hills when an old lady . . . over eighty . . . a relative-in-law . . . stole in.
>
> "I say dearie," she began in a whisper bending down to my face, "would you mind if I was to sit in the corner over there . . . and listen to your talk after Miss Cummins comes. . . . I never had a chance to hear two actresses talk before and I may never have another."
>
> . . . She took up her position just in time to escape being seen by the incoming guests. We, (Maria Cummins and I) chatted away cheerily at our far window watching the sunset. . . .
>
> "Summer sunsets are associated in my mind in a dreamy way with the tinkle of cow bells," observed my companion and went on to tell how as a child living in Salem she used to watch the long line of cows coming in from the meadows at night and how

musically the tinkle of many bells blended with the other sunset sounds.

I have the same association with my Virginia home I answered, so had Gray with Stoke Pogis. But his herd lowed as it wound slowly over the lea.

"Perhaps English cows are hungrier than ours," Miss Cummins followed in a like strain. . . .

The unseen listener carried off upstairs but one impression of the actresses . . . and was grievously disappointed. We had talked of nothing but cows and cowbells and cows coming home hungry for supper and such stuff. "For all the world as if they had lived on a dairy farm all their days."

Unwittingly perhaps, the aged eavesdropper had put her finger on one secret of success the two novelists shared—the ability to find drama in the commonplace, the skill to select the detail and incident that create realism.

The Lamplighter took its title from the profession of a kind old man, Trueman Flint, who rescued Gerty, a little orphan, from the streets, but he did not live long enough to occupy a very important role. The story belonged to Gerty, who became the indispensable woman, equally competent in affairs temporal or spiritual.

Quite early in the story a neighbor told her, "You never have been taught to do anything, my child, but a girl eight years old can do many things if she is patient and tries to learn." The future existence of Gerty, a larger, bolder, stronger Fleda, elaborated this theme.

At eight she cleaned, cooked and in general managed her benefactor's home. After he was disabled she nursed him until he died and then went on to become the companion and solace of a young blind woman, Miss Emily. When Gerty's childhood sweetheart, Willie, left for India, she assumed the responsibility of *his* family, attended *his* ill mother and insane grandmother.

But where Fleda had been content to work her miracles with a deprecating air, to function behind the scenes, to be modestly unassuming in her triumphs and to resign her position and gains into the rather incompetent hands of her uncle when he reappeared on the scene, Gerty was blunt, obvious and self-assertive. Where Fleda glided in and out, Gerty stamped. Somewhere along the way Gerty acquired an excellent education which enabled her to teach school for pay— while unofficially instructing the general public gratis. Her dress, manner and conduct provided a salutary example to every woman, an immediate inspiration to every man she met. If possible her moral strength surpassed even her mental prowess and physical stamina. She softened a worldly sinner (later discovered to be her long-lost father) merely by dropping a tear on his face as he slept.

She particularly excelled in the field of self-sacrifice. She discovered, nursed and forgave the old woman who treated her so cruelly as a child. She resigned her sweetheart, Willie, to another without consulting him. Trapped in a flaming steamboat, she insisted that her most bitter persecutor should be saved first.

On and on as the book progressed, Gerty rose to new moral pinnacles while her associates sank beneath the ever-increasing burden of gratitude they owed her. At last, all misunderstandings resolved, she was united with Willie, her childhood sweetheart, "amid the familiar beauties of a cemetery she often frequented."

All the Happy Endings

The Lamplighter ended in a graveyard. *Alone* began in one, as the heroine's mother was buried. The bereaved daughter, an orphan, who prepared to take up her residence in the home of an unsympathetic guardian, was, like the author, a sixteen-year-old girl and, in common with many adolescents, humorless, self-conscious and ungracious, by turns sulky, moody or bitter, given to unfounded suspicions, sudden withdrawals and rather senseless attachments. It is hard to understand what identification readers could have found in this disagreeable girl unless they too shared her feeling of being constantly misunderstood, unloved and persecuted.

The locale of *Alone*, the environs of Richmond, where servants abounded, limited Ida Ross's opportunities to perfect herself in quite as many everyday skills as Fleda and Gerty but she proved equally adept at saving souls—beginning with her own. About halfway through *Alone* the heroine, disappointed in love, turned after a great inner struggle from an "acquiescent Christian" to an ardent, practicing, believing one.

So fortified, she learned to manage people and control situations, to be the unchanging star about which the lesser galaxy revolved. She soothed deathbeds, silenced gossip, reprimanded flirts, reformed rakes, saved marriages, dispensed charity, confounded skeptics and did good for evil so persistently that her guardian, subjected to her ministrations throughout his last illness, exclaimed:

I hated you from the minute you entered this house, and you repaid me with compound interest. Here you are, sitting up at night; waiting on me all day. I can't do without you, because you are handy and wakeful, but I don't like you. Do you hear?

102

Ida Ross did not need words, or even tears, to save souls—example sufficed. "*You* were the beginning," the last heathen in her circle told Ida as he stepped forward to lead the prayer service," . . . the consistent practice of one private Christian did more to convict me than the preaching of the entire apostolic succession—Saints Paul and Peter to head them—could have done."

"Whether or not," Marion Harland wrote her friend "Effie" (Miss Virginia Eppes Dance) when *Alone* appeared, "others may cavil at the religious tone and ridicule the simplicity of the narrative remains to be seen."

No one did. There were sound reasons why talk of conversion, religious experience, spiritual influence assumed great importance not only to Marion Harland but to all women of the period. The principle that before God all men were spiritually equal and might without intermediaries communicate directly with their Maker was a basic concept of the early Protestant Reformation in Europe. Among the Waldenses and Cathars members of both sexes might preach, but after the Lutheran and Calvinist compromise it was not always clear that "man" included woman as well.

Certainly the clerical oligarchy that controlled early Puritan America gave women a subordinate place in the family and none at all in politics or the church. Anyone inclined to disagree publicly with this rule must have first pondered the fate of Anne Hutchinson, whose temerity in questioning the colonial divines led to her banishment from the Bay Colony in 1638. In the eighth month of her pregnancy, holding her four-year-old daughter by the hand, Anne Hutchinson walked from Boston through snow, ice and March thaw to the safety of Roger Williams' settlement in Rhode Island. Her miscarriage, after her arrival in Providence, was declared by the Reverend John Cotton of Boston to be but a just punishment for her heresy.

Whether the women of his congregation concurred is not recorded, for Anne Hutchinson's trial served its purpose and during the next 150 years women in colonial America followed the advice of St. Paul and, covering their heads, kept silence in the house of the Lord.

Gradually new settlements by people with varying religious beliefs made greater tolerance an economic and political necessity. Groups with strong equalitarian principles, such as the Friends, the Moravians, the Anabaptists, exerted a liberalizing influence beyond their own congregations. As the struggle for political liberty intensified, so, too, did the desire for religious freedom. The formal church with a clerical hierarchy and rigid discipline did not adapt to the special conditions of the frontier—long distances, isolated communities, scattered families, the hard and constant struggle for existence. The lack of facilities in the new country for training a sufficient body of clergy also encouraged the growth of denominations (the Methodists, Baptists, Disciples and others) using lay preachers or leaders, circuit riders or missionaries.

Increasingly communication with the Divine Being, understanding His will, receiving His grace, furthering His kingdom on earth became matters of individual concern. The wave of revivalism that began early in the eighteenth century and reached its crest in the camp meetings of the thirties and forties indicated the shift of religion from a spiritual or rational conviction limited to a select number to an emotional experience available to all.

Women soon took advantage of the situation. The church as an institution might still belong to men but, if the direct way to God was free to all, then intuition equaled doctrine, spirit was as valuable as liturgy, innocence surpassed knowledge, and the touch of a good woman's hand, the glistening tear from her brimming eye might be better equipment for soul saving than a theological degree from Harvard.

The "silence" was broken by a chorus of feminine voices, explaining and interpreting the Divine mysteries. This represented another of the several common interests Mrs. Catherine Palmer Putnam and Susan Warner shared with each other and with the women of their time. Scarcely had the ink dried on *Queechy*'s pages before Susan Warner offered her readers *The Law and the Testimony*, "a collection of passages in the Bible having a bearing upon . . . points of doctrine such as the Divine Nature, Divinity of the Saviour, God's Omniscience and etc."

Mrs. Putnam symbolized the growing power of her sex in theological matters by literally appropriating a church. Brought up in the Congregational faith, she joined the Baptists in early life and, though she retained membership in that denomination, subsequently embraced many Swedenborgian views. She wrote her own commentary on the Old Testament. When some of her ideas proved unacceptable to fellow Baptists in Brunswick, Maine, she seceded and, taking a considerable part of the congregation with her, formed a second Baptist church. It is a testimonial to her personality, if not to her theology, that *her* church continued until she left Brunswick, whereupon the members quietly rejoined the original Baptist group.

Salvation, women were not slow to discover, offered practical as well as spiritual benefits, a point clearly illustrated in the story of Susan Warner's conversion, shortly after her father's failure. As Anna Warner described it

walking up Waverly Place one day, she [Susan] met an acquaintance who just then was counted a leader of fashion. And as they passed, this woman's bow was so slight and cool that it almost had the air of a rebuff. Whether so meant or not does not matter it seemed so to my sister. And as she walked on with that sense of check that is so painful to a young person, all her nerves astir at the supposed slight, she said in her heart that she would put her happiness in a safer place, beyond the reach of scornful fingers.

Two weeks later Susan Warner joined the church. Here was no soul-shaking struggle—no mystic union, no glimpse of eternal glory—the "communion of Saints" had become the superior social set.

Women derived other advantages in becoming one of the heavenly elite. The decisions of a husband, a father, a clergyman were no longer absolute but might be referred directly to a Higher Power who began, rather belatedly, to render verdicts favoring the feminine sex. If men questioned this manifestation of Divine Will, personally revealed, they found unruly wives and disobedient daughters transformed into persecuted martyrs.

In *The Wide, Wide World* little Ellen often escaped the control of her aunt and later her uncle on the grounds that their wishes and desires for her ran counter to a Higher

Authority. Gerty at sixteen could defy her guardian with "I will never be a traitor to my own heart and my sense of right. Having thus committed her cause to Him who judgeth righteously, Gertrude tried to compose herself to sleep."

To find and to know God, to interpret His will, to further His kingdom no longer required theological training, a knowledge of Greek and Hebrew; inspiration, intuition, spirit, sensibility served instead. Females, since they admittedly excelled in these qualities, seemed especially ordained to be the exclusive keepers of the Keys to Heaven.

If proof were wanted of the magic power, the far-reaching influence of good woman over wicked man, the curious story of the success of Marion Harland's *Alone* would provide it. The book had a rather inauspicious start. Morris, the Richmond bookseller to whom it was submitted, declined to risk publication until Marion Harland's father agreed to assume the costs. The book's circulation might have been confined to the locality except for a strange circumstance described later by Marion Harland in her autobiography:

Alone had been out in the world about three months, when I received a letter from a stranger, postmarked "Baltimore", and bearing the letter-head of a daily paper published in that city. The signature was "James Redpath." The writer related briefly that, chancing to go into Morris' book-store while on a visit to Richmond, he had had from the publisher a copy of my book, and read it. He went on to say:

"It is full of faults, as you will discover for yourself in time. Personally, I may remark, that I detest both your politics and your theology. All the same, you will make your mark upon the age. In the full persuasion of this, I write to pledge myself to do all in my power to forward your literary interests. I am not on the staff of the Baltimore paper, although now visiting the editor-in-chief. But I have influence in more than one quarter, and you will hear from me again."

I laid the queer epistle before my father, and we agreed that my outspoken critic was slightly demented. . . .

I was therefore unprepared for the strenuous manner in which Mr. James Redpath proceeded to keep his pledge. Not a week passed in which he did not send me a clipping from some paper, containing a direct or incidental notice of my book, or work, or personality. Now he was in New Orleans, writing fiery Southern editorials, and insinuating into the body of same, adroit mention of the rising Southern author. Now he slipped into a Cincinnati paper a poem taken from Alone, with a line or two, calling attention to the novel and the author; then a fierce attack upon the "detested politics and theology" flamed among book notices in a Buffalo journal, tempered by regrets that "real talent should be grossly perverted by sectional prejudice and superstition." Anon, a clever review in a Boston paper pleased my friends in the classic city so much that they sent a marked copy to me, not dreaming that I had already had the critique with the now familiar "J.R." scrawled in the margin . . .

Eventually after several other notices appeared, Marion Harland wrote and expressed her gratitude and as she said:

confessed my inability to divine the motive power of benefactions so numerous and unsolicited. Redpath's reply deepened the mystery:

"Your book held me back from infidelity, Chapter Sixteen saved my life. Now that you know thus much, we will, if you please, have no more talk on your part of gratitude."

Five years elapsed between the receipt of that first note signed "James Redpath", and the explanation of what followed. I may relate here, in a few sentences, what he wrote to me at length, and what was published in an appreciative biographical sketch written by a personal friend after his death.

. . . Disappointed in certain enterprises upon which he had fixed his mind and expended his best energies, he found himself in Richmond, with but one purpose in his soul. He would be lost to all who knew him, and leave no trace of the failure he believed himself to be. He put a pistol in his pocket and set out for Hollywood Cemetery. There were sequestered glens there, then, and lonely thickets into which a world-beaten man could crawl to die. On the way up-town he stopped at the bookstore and fell into talk with the proprietor, who, on learning the stranger's profession, handed him the lately-published novel. Arrived at the cemetery, Redpath was disappointed to see the roads and paths gay with carriages, pedestrians and riding-parties. He would wait until twilight sent them back to town. He lay down upon the turf on a knoll commanding a view of the beautiful city and the river, took out his book and began reading to while away the hours that would bring quiet and solitude. The sun was high, still. He had the editorial knack of rapid reading. The dew was beginning to fall as he finished the narrative of the interrupted duel in the sixteenth chapter.

Before he slept that night he registered a vow—thus he phrased it in his explanatory letter—to write and publish one thousand notices of the book that had saved his life.

Redpath kept his vow and a master of modern publicity methods could have done no more to ensure the book's success.

Grace Greenwood, whose brilliant literary letters had great influence with the reading public, expressed her admiration for the novel. Henry Longfellow wrote his enthusiasm, adding that Mrs. Longfellow "was reading Alone in her turn."

New editions and reprints appeared, followed by publication in England and on the Continent and an eventual sale of more than a hundred thousand copies.

Who now could doubt the power of women?

9   A New Heroine—
and Hero

After the publication of *Retribution* in 1849 scarcely a year passed without one, sometimes two new works from the pen of Mrs. E. D. E. N. Southworth and her name became a household word, almost a trade-mark for that peculiar form of fiction, the domestic novel.

Her initials were not, as many supposed, a romantic invention. Mrs. Southworth, born in Washington, D. C., in 1819, had actually been baptized Emma Dorothy Eliza at the bedside of the dying father, Captain Charles Nevitte.

Her early life as she described it in an autobiographical sketch was not a happy one.

I was a child of sorrow from the very first year of my life. Thin and dark, I had no beauty except a pair of large, wild eyes—but even this was destined to be tarnished. At twelve months I was attacked with an inflammation of the eyes, that ended in total, though happily temporary, blindness . . . At three years of age my sight began to clear. About this time my only sister was born. . . .

. . . a very beautiful child, with fair and rounded form, rosy complexion, soft blue eyes, and golden hair. . . . She was of a lively, social, loving nature, and, as she grew, won all hearts around her—parents, cousins, nurses, servants, and all who had been wearied to death with two year's attendance on such a weird

110

little elf as myself—yes, and who made me feel it, too.

I was wildly, passionately attached to my father, and even his partiality in favor of my younger sister—his "dove-eyed darling" as he called her, did not affect my love for him. But he was often from home for months at a time, and all my life was then divided into two periods—when he was gone; when he was home; and every event dated from one of two epochs—joyfully, "since father came home;" sadly, "since father went away." But at last my father who had never recovered from the effects of his wound acquired during the War of 1812 got a cold, which fell upon his lungs. His health declined rapidly. Someone—I know not who—came and said, "Emma, your father is dead." I remember I felt as if I had received a sudden, stunning blow upon the brow. I reeled back from the blow an instant, unable to meet it, and then, with an impulse to escape the calamity turned and fled— fled with my utmost speed, until, at some distance from home, I fell upon my face exhausted, insensible. . . . For months, even years afterward, I ruminated on life, death, heaven and hell with a painful intensity of thought impossible to describe.

At the age of six I was a little, thin, dark, wild-eyed elf, shy, awkward, and unattractive and, in consequence, very much let alone. I spent much time in solitude, revery, or mischief; took to attics, cellars, and cocklofts, consorting with cats and pigeons, or with the old negroes in the kitchen, listening with open ears and mind to ghost stories, old legends, and tales of the time when "Ole Mist'ess was rich and saw lots of grand company"—very happy when I could get my little sister to share my queer pleasures; but "Lotty" was a parlor favorite, and was better pleased with the happy faces of our young country cousins, some of whom were always with us on long visits.

Three years after Captain Nevitte's death his young widow married Joshua Henshaw of Boston who had first come to the Capital as Daniel Webster's secretary and later opened a school in Washington. There Emma, by her own admission a most difficult pupil—and stepdaughter—was educated.

> At this time of my life, rejoicing in the light and liberty of nature I should have been very happy also in the love of my friends and relations, if they had permitted it; but no matter! Year after year, from my eighth to my sixteenth year I grew more lonely, retired more into myself, until, notwithstanding a strong, ardent, demonstrative temperament, I became cold, reserved and abstracted, even to absence of mind—even to apparent insensibility.

After her graduation at sixteen she taught school until, four years later, she met and married Frederick H. Southworth and went with him to Prairie du Chien, Wisconsin. In 1844 she was back in Washington again with two little children and no husband. Friends secured her appointment as a teacher in the Fourth District Primary School. Her salary, $250 a year, scarcely supported her family and on Christmas Eve, 1844, alone, dispirited, tired, poor, she sat down and wrote a short story, "The Irish Refugee." She took it to Shillington's Book Shop where she frequently browsed among the volumes her poverty did not permit her to buy and asked the proprietor to send the manuscript to one of the magazines he stocked. Joe Shillington good-humoredly obliged. When the *Baltimore Sunday Visitor*'s acceptance came, no one in the shop knew the author's name or address. Eventually, Mrs. Southworth stopped in again, learned the news and also the deflating fact that the *Visitor* did not pay for contributions. However, the editor did call her work to the attention of Dr. Gamaliel Bailey of the *National Era*, and he published her next story, *The Better Way, or The Wife's Victory.*

Through Dr. Bailey Mrs. Southworth met John Greenleaf Whittier and the two became fast friends. Mrs. Southworth, from her storehouse of Maryland tales and traditions, gave Whittier the idea for his poem, "Barbara Frietchie." Whittier in his turn suggested to Dr. Bailey that Mrs. Southworth become a regular contributor to the *Era*. Six short stories and her first full-length novel, *Retribution*, appeared there.

Retribution, when published in book form by Harper's in 1849, received excellent notices and brought Mrs. Southworth an offer to contribute to the *Saturday Evening Post*. She resigned her teaching position and during the next seven years wrote twelve full-length novels; the *Era* serialized four, the *Post*, eight. All when published as books won laudatory reviews. The *Saturday Visitor* called Mrs. Southworth's second book, *The Deserted Wife*, "The very best story now in course of publication in this country written by the very best writer this country claims." The demand for her third, *The Mother-In-Law*, proved so great that the *Post* twice reprinted editions of the earlier chapters to supply new subscribers.

Novel followed novel. In rapid succession appeared *The Three Beauties, The Two Sisters, The Discarded Daughter, The Curse of Clifton, India: The Pearl of Pearl River, The Lost Heiress, The Missing Bride, The Brothers, Vivia,* and with each the author's popularity increased.

"Mrs. Southworth is considered the finest authoress in the country," the New York *Mirror* declared; "one of the very first female writers of the age," the New York *Ledger* agreed.

The reviewer on *Graham's Magazine*, who said he could not discover "one passage of true feeling, humor or pathos" in *The Curse of Clifton*, found himself in sad minority. The

New Literary World judged the book "worthy of Currer Bell"; the *Post*, prejudiced, perhaps, in favor of their star contributor, proclaimed that Mrs. Southworth, "equal to Dickens and superior to Emily Brontë, reminded one of Shakespeare." The *Post*'s circulation increased. The leading publishers bid for book publication on new work, reprint permissions on the old.

Undoubtedly Mrs. Southworth did possess many of the qualities that make a good storyteller. She was imaginative, impressionable, inventive. "There are incidents enough in any one of your stories," Mrs. Harriet Beecher Stowe once told her, "to supply a half dozen novels." Mrs. Southworth had a strong sense of drama; she delighted in color and motion —in contrasts of scene and character. With her readers she shared a taste for the sensational, the violent, the supernatural, the macabre, the mysterious. She knew how to combine the shock and suspense of the old Gothic novel with the pathos, sentiment and humor Dickens and his imitators had made fashionable.

Unlike the majority of her contemporaries who attributed human depravity to the individual's willful and deliberate choice, Mrs. Southworth perceived that more complex and cumulative factors might be involved in personality development. She could understand the crime motivated by passion or immediate need. Despite some small snobberies—she shared the democratic ideal. She hated injustice and sympathized with its victims, the poor, the illegitimate, the abused child, the mistreated slave, the overworked servant, the neglected orphan and—most of all—the deserted wife.

In public biography and private conversation Mrs. Southworth revealed very little about her own broken marriage, writing only:

Let me pass over in silence the stormy and disastrous days of my wretched girlhood, days that stamped upon my brow of youth the furrows of fifty years—let me come at once to the time when I found myself broken in spirit, health, and purse —a widow in fate, but not in fact.

In her novels, however, Mrs. Southworth was not so reticent. Over and over in plot, subplot, and incident she introduced the wife deserted for good or evil reasons and destined by fate, coincidence, accident or plan to make her way in the world.

Mrs. Hentz maimed the husband. Mrs. Southworth removed him entirely. This plan had several advantages. A martyred wife deserved and usually won the sympathy and approval of her circle. She had the prestige even a poor marriage conferred, with few of the responsibilities. She had control of her person, her children, her earnings. She had, if she were circumspect, almost complete freedom of action. When her wanderer finally returned, as he always did abject and repentant, she enjoyed a day of justification and glory and a lifetime of moral superiority.

Retribution's heroine died leaving her unfaithful husband to his own guilty conscience, but Mrs. Southworth never made this mistake again. In her second book, *The Deserted Wife*, Hagar was made of stronger stuff. When *her* husband ran away with a pretty, compliant young woman (later rather shockingly discovered to be his long-lost sister), Hagar, penniless and near death, turned to the concert stage to sup-

115

port her three children. There she won honors, ovations and a handsome fortune. At the moment of her greatest triumph her erring husband, permitted a glimpse of her surrounded by adoring crowds and applauded by royalty, sought her out to confess:

"Hagar! I have not one word to say for myself! Not one excuse to offer for my weakness! Not one syllable to breathe in palliation of my fault! Hagar, I am a bankrupt!"

Words the heroine and apparently the writer and her readers longed to hear. For through ninety volumes Mrs. Southworth dreamed, and millions of women dreamed with her, the recurring dream: I loved him; I trusted him; I gave him everything—and for what? I was ignored, scorned, betrayed, rejected, but he will come back and yearn for what he cast so lightly away.

In Mrs. Southworth's novels those husbands who did not desert their wives went off to the wars, the legislature, the far West or some equally remote corner of the world and stayed there until needed for the dramatic reunion in the closing chapter with their respective, and always competent, wives.

When Mrs. Southworth exhausted all possible ways of removing a husband, she sometimes varied the situation by removing the wife—admittedly more difficult to manage without violating custom. In *The Discarded Daughter* the wife had to submit patiently to her husband's rages, threats, physical violence, his seizure of all her property and personal possessions, and not until this monster buried her alive did the long-suffering woman feel justified in leaving him. Short of equal provocation any deserting wife ran the risk of losing the moral advantage.

Mrs. Southworth also had wives abducted by wicked guardians, brigands, or rejected suitors, cast on desert islands, and lost in impenetrable wilderness. In these situations unprotected women exerted over their male companions the same power that enables virgins to tame unicorns. Only husbands, actual or potential, ever attempted to assault females.

Mrs. Southworth introduced another way to be "a wife in name only," the child bride. Economic necessity made early marriage common in the United States. Travelers from abroad noted, with surprise, mothers at fifteen, grandmothers at thirty, often with partners several years their senior. Mrs. Southworth's own mother at fifteen had married a man of forty-five. Frequent childbearing and the hardships of the frontier exacted a severe toll and the graves of four, five, sometimes more, "loving spouses" flanked a patriarch's tomb.

Mrs. Southworth's child brides were the pampered, petted darlings of compliant and undemanding old men—with a comfortable, independent widowhood in reversion. In *The Curse of Clifton*, Mrs. Southworth drew such a couple:

". . . I am too old for you. Georgia—I know it, alas! too well, now that it is too late—and yet you did not raise the least objection to becoming my wife, Georgia."

"Ha! ha! ha! . . . *Objection*! I was but fifteen years of age when you bribed me to your arms with a set of jewels, and a gold mounted work-box! I was a child, delighted with glittering toys! and fond, yes! *very* fond of the grandfatherly old man that poured them into my lap! Did *that* child-fondness deceive you?"

"It did, it did! . . . Georgia, I am an old man, as you justly said—*quite* an old man. I have not very long to live, and when I die, Georgia, you will still be a very young woman . . . in ten years you will be but twenty-seven, and is it even likely that I shall live so long as that? No! And after my heart is cold, and my head is laid low, Georgia will be a beautiful young widow —ay, and with a rich jointure, too! I shall take care of that!"

Readers apparently saw nothing unwholesome in such a match. Mrs. Hale of *Godey's* thought the characters "skillfully drawn and true to nature." *The Curse of Clifton* proved one of Mrs. Southworth's most popular books, and it joined *Uncle Tom's Cabin* and Charles Dickens' *Bleak House* as one of 1852's three best-selling fiction titles.

Despite her success, Mrs. Southworth found it difficult to support her household, educate her children and help her relatives on her earnings. The *Post* paid her somewhat more than the *Era*'s $10-a-column rate but Peterson, who purchased the copyright and reissued several of her earlier novels, drove a notoriously hard bargain and she admitted that in her dealings with other houses she had "not one bit of business tact."

As early as 1848 her health, never robust, began to decline. She wrote on. Her son, Richmond, contracted an illness diagnosed as incurable—the weekly chapter still had to be done. Richmond and his sister, Charlotte, caught scarlet fever and no nurse could be found—Mrs. Southworth brought her desk to their bedside. Her eyesight failed—she dictated the required installment. The next years brought new trouble. She wrote a letter to her readers which the *Post* published:

But may God in His mercy save us forevermore from such trouble as visited our home during the two successive years, in which "The Lost Heiress" and "Miriam" were written. It is a marvel to me yet, how either of those works were ever completed. The worst of what we suffered I will not even hint to you, because it implicates others whom I would much prefer to leave to the sure judgement of God. But beside our greatest sorrow, sickness, death, litigation, the parting from friends identified with our lives—all followed in close succession, until I am almost tempted to believe that the evil destinies had received full permission to test the full strength of my human heart.

This was not all. Her relations with the *Post* grew strained. They wanted shorter novels, complete in ten or twelve issues. Mrs. Southworth promised and tried but her next serial, *The Lost Heiress,* ran to twenty-nine installments, after that came *Miriam* in thirty-five, followed by *Vivia* in thirty-nine.

How readers could retain from week to week, year to year the involved plots and complicated interrelation of the characters in Mrs. Southworth's books is a mystery greater than any she wrote. In *Vivia* double cousins, half sisters, uncles, guardians, brothers, husbands, both first and second, and assorted mothers, step, foster, spurious and long lost, crowded her pages. In this novel the inevitable deserted wife became a nun and her lost husband a Jesuit providing several glimpses, all sympathetic, of convent life, rather a daring novelty in the year of the Know-Nothing party's greatest popularity.

Mrs. Southworth, an Episcopalian with some Swedenborgian views and a romantic interest in Catholicism, never exhibited the patent piety of the other domestic novelists. "Sweet and beautiful and lovely as is the deathbed of a Christian," Mrs. Southworth wrote in *The Hidden Hand,* "we will not linger too long beside it." On this principle her heroines, hastening from adventure to adventure while acknowledging

119

a Divine Being, recognizing His particular protection, relied on themselves.

If they had a theology, it was one rather personally their own. In *Vivia* that young lady was "the medium of animating, sustaining or redeeming life to all within her sphere . . . when once asked the secret of her power she answered boldly, 'Faith'."

She urged her friends:

"Believe it—believe it! Have faith. By faith you shall remove mountains, cure diseases, cast out devils, raise the dead . . ."

Vivia's "Faith" seemed not so much faith in God or faith in herself as just faith in Faith—a kind of militant optimism, peculiarly American, in which to want and to believe and to expect and to deserve equaled to receive.

Vivia's author, meantime, sorely needed some of this magic power to solve her own problems. The doctor diagnosed Mrs. Southworth's continuing illness as tuberculosis and gave her three months to live. She wrote later:

I was dying from the combined effect of overwork and under pay, of anxiety, of actual privation. When my doctor told me of a diet necessary to the restoration of my health I was obliged to reply to him that I could not afford it—and so I could not.

To her rescue at this desperate moment came a shrewd, young Scotch-Irish immigrant named Robert Bonner with an interesting business offer which Mrs. Southworth accepted and in her own words:

That night of storm and darkness came to an end, and morning broke on me at last, a bright glad morning, pioneering a new and happy day of life. First of all it was in this tempest of trouble that my "life sorrow" was, as it were carried away, or I was carried away from brooding over it. Next my child contrary to my own opinion and the Doctor's got well . . . friends crowded around me, offers for contributions poured in upon me and I, who . . . had been poor, ill, forsaken, slandered, killed by sorrow, privation, toil and friendlessness found myself born into a new life, found independence, sympathy, friendship and honor and an occupation in which I could delight.

Robert Bonner, as a boy of fifteen, came from Ramelton, Northern Ireland, in 1839 to work on his uncle's Connecticut farm. Before long he found a place on the Hartford *Courant* and mastering the printer's trade moved on to New York. After a stint on the *American Republican,* Bonner joined the New York *Mirror,* where N. P. Willis, the controversial editor, let his new typesetter try his hand at some writing and editing. Four years later Bonner acquired his own press and began printing the New York *Ledger* for its proprietors and in 1851 assumed entire control of the paper. It ran little but financial, business and legal notices and advertisements but Bonner, then twenty-six, had great plans for his new property. He wanted to make it the most popular family fiction magazine in the world, and he knew, further, exactly how to go about achieving his goal.

The idea of a story paper did not originate with Bonner. Several already courted the new reader—*Uncle Sam,* the Boston *Notion,* the *Saturday Evening Post,* the Philadelphia *Saturday Courier,* the *Olive Branch,* the *Flag of Our Union.* The last-named, perhaps the most successful, had established a precedent by omitting all advertising and buying its fiction

121

from native authors, among them T. S. Arthur, Horatio Alger, Sylvanus Cobb, Mrs. Lydia Sigourney, Ann Stephens, Edgar Allan Poe, and Edward Z. C. Judson, who, as Ned Buntline, turned William Cody, nondescript Indian fighter, into Buffalo Bill, American folk hero.

To this highly competitive field Bonner brought singular gifts. He was shrewd, inventive, daring, with that special knack for creating and using publicity which only those with a sure sense of public taste possess. All the aggressive energy, the temperate habits, the moral convictions his age held dear were his together with the ability to make these virtues produce a profit.

A strict Presbyterian, an elder in his church, he neither drank, smoked nor cursed and boasted he did not know the number of cards in a deck. Passionately interested in horses, he spent more than a quarter million dollars on blooded stock. "God made fast horses, so I shall let them run," he said, but he never bet on a race.

He made munificent contributions to charity, to Princeton, to his own church, to other worthy denominations and to deserving clergymen. He commissioned twelve ministers to write a novel each for the *Ledger*. To one of them, Henry Ward Beecher, he paid $30,000 for *Norwood*, a work so bad that the divine himself laughingly confessed that many people believed he was the real author of *Uncle Tom's Cabin* until *Norwood* convinced them he was not. But the Beecher name, Bonner estimated, brought in $120,000 in new business and the presence of the other clerical worthies helped the magazine achieve respectability in many quarters.

Bonner's patriotism, and he was sincerely devoted to his

adopted country—"we are all sovereigns here," he said proudly —produced a profitable return when he lured the great Edward Everett (a former president of Harvard and a one-time minister to the Court of St. James's) to the *Ledger's* pages with a $10,000 fee for a series on the restoration of Mount Vernon.

Realizing the appeal of names, Bonner paid Tennyson $5,000 for a single poem, ordered an original story from Charles Dickens and eventually numbered among his contributors Henry Wadsworth Longfellow, William Cullen Bryant, Lydia Maria Child, Mrs. Horace Mann, Horace Greeley, James Gordon Bennett, George Bancroft, and United States senators and college presidents by the dozens.

Bonner, who shunned all personal publicty, received only intimates in his home, disliked being photographed and never allowed a single line of advertising in the *Ledger,* made advertising history and achieved his first publishing coup when in 1855 he engaged Fanny Fern, daughter of Nathaniel Willis, editor of the *Youth's Companion* and sister of N. P. Willis of the New York *Mirorr,* to write him a story at the astounding rate of $100 per column. While other papers inquired editorially if this were insanity or stupidity, Bonner took whole pages in the metropolitan dailies to run the single line, repeated over and over and over: "Fanny Fern writes for the New York Ledger." The investment soon returned a handsome profit in new subscribers eager to see this expensive talent at work.

Fanny Fern, born Sarah Payson Willis, in Portland, Maine, in 1811, was a problem girl from the time she attended Miss Catharine Beecher's Seminary at Hartford, Connecticut, where she flouted Miss Harriet Beecher, then a student teacher, tore pages from her Euclid to use for curl papers, ran up bills in the town candy shop and flirted with the youthful Henry Ward Beecher.

After two marriages, the second ending in divorce, with two children to support and no money, Fanny appealed to her brother, N. P. Willis, for help in starting a literary career. He curtly advised her, or so she said, to make shirts for a living. Instead Sarah Willis Eldredge Farrington, adopting a pseudonym and style not unlike that of her brother's protégé, Fanny Forrester, began contributing to the *Olive Branch*. Her sketches, terse and timely, contained sentiment, wit, pathos and venom in just the right proportions to charm readers, and soon newspapers all over the country began copying her work. J. C. Derby of Derby and Miller, sensing a best seller, arranged to publish a collection and the book, *Fern Leaves*, sold almost a hundred thousand copies and brought the author $10,000. Similar volumes followed which did almost as well and at the height of this popularity Fanny accepted Bonner's offer.

Her first effort for him, a serial, *Fanny Ford, A Story of Everyday Life*, had little merit and despite the publicity it achieved was not published in book form for several years.

Fanny Fern had never forgiven her brother and in her next novel, *Ruth Hall*, she told the whole story of the Willis family feud. Readers, finding it easy and exciting to identify the thinly disguised characters, bought 50,000 copies in the first eight months after publication.

Enough interest in Fanny Fern's work persisted to give her *Rose Clark*, published the following year, a comfortable sale. But Fanny had run out of grievances. It was only her brother, not the whole male sex, she wanted to discipline, and that same year, 1856, she married her third and last husband, James Parton, and devoted herself entirely to writing sketches for the *Ledger* and, as she said, "hitting folly as it flies."

Meantime Bonner, who early recognized Fanny Fern's limitations as a novelist and serialized only her first book, was looking around for competent workers. Novel ideas might catch readers, but to hold them a paper required a reliable supply of sensational fiction. Bonner knew this and raided Ballou's *Flag of Our Union,* and with an offer of higher rates took their star, Sylvanus Cobb. To advertise his new contributor's first story for the *Ledger—The Gun Makers of Moscow* —Bonner spent $20,000 and had a hundred gun salute fired in City Hall Park.

The "woman's touch" was still lacking and in the fall of 1856 Bonner went to Mrs. Southworth and offered her the $40 a week that "saved her life." In return for this she agreed to write a twenty-page installment on a serial novel and to work for no other American periodical.

Bonner spent $27,000 to advertise *The Island Princess,* Mrs. Southworth's first story for the *Ledger,* which began on May 30, 1857, and was later published as *The Lady of the Isle.* She followed this the next year with an old, though hitherto unpublished story, *The Bride of an Evening.* Both came from a tired pen.

But Bonner showed his confidence in his new contributor by increasing her weekly stipend to $50 and further undertook to deal with her publisher, T. B. Peterson of Philadelphia, on book rights to her *Ledger* serials.

125

"Peterson won't give any more than he can help," Mrs. Southworth wrote her new friend. "Do your best for me."

Bonner did, and sustained by his friendship and advice, Mrs. Southworth began one of the most popular books she ever wrote, *Capitola; or, The Hidden Hand,* the tale of a street waif, rescued and adopted by an elderly relative. The serial enjoyed an immediate and an enormous success. Women wore Capitola hats and suits in honor of the heroine. Towns, boats, and hotels appropriated her magic name.

Forty dramatic versions were made—one or more eventually played in almost every city in the United States. Three crowded London theaters all offered *Capitola,* and when Mrs. Southworth and her children visited England in 1861 she saw John Wilkes Booth as the brigand, Black Donald.

In *Capitola* as in *Vivia,* long-lost relatives discovered each other with monotonous regularity. Several complicated subplots arose from the machinations of a villain, Le Noir, who murdered his brother, imprisoned his sister-in-law in a madhouse, abducted their child and its nurse, sold them into slavery, confiscated the estate, mistreated his ward and schemed to have her fiancé dishonored and sentenced to death by a court-martial. All this, understandably, provided action and well-sustained suspense but the book's real attraction was Capitola, a new kind of heroine.

In the early decades of the nineteenth century, when "praise to the face was an open disgrace" and "handsome was as handsome did," authors wasted little beauty on their heroines. It was enough for Charlotte Temple to be "a tall elegant girl" with blue eyes to match her bonnet and a habit of blushing, while in *The Coquette* "agreeable manners and refined talents" made Eliza Wharton the toast of her county. During the forties and early fifties the meek gentle doves who glided through the pages of the novels were drawn to a single pattern—brow and hair smooth, eyes and head drooping, rosebud mouth pursed. Fanny Forrester made a composite picture of them all in her description of Dora in a story of the same name:

. . . eyes like a wet violet nestled among the profusion of the softest hued Persian fringes and hair from the elfin fields of Erin and combed and twisted by fairy fingers. Then those lips with their sad sweetness and the love thought in each corner! And the pale polished cheek and vein crossed forehead . . . step like a fawns, a head . . . like a wild deer on the lookout for the huntsman . . . a face full of half joyous, half solemn surprise such as Eve must have worn when her foot first crushed the dews and flowers of Eden.

The "pale polished cheeks," the general fragility, unfortunately far too common among women of the period, frequently betokened serious physical disorders. America, even well into the nineteenth century, was a notoriously unhealthy place. Fevers, agues, rheumatism, dyspepsia, flux were chronic national complaints. Yet the fecundity rate was the highest ever recorded, and thus doubly burdened many wives died long before their husbands.

Travelers from abroad usually noted that all American women faded early. Prone to headaches, fainting fits, hysteria, nervous debility, green sickness and the decline, they dosed themselves with laudanum, strong tea and alchoholic "tonic." At thirty they were worn, at forty, old.

After the middle of the century general health standards

slowly rose owing to increased scientific knowledge, better sanitation practices, and more medical schools to train doctors. About the same time the typically American version of the ideal woman that still exists began to emerge.

The aches and pains of women were not imaginary and so they did not immediately disappear. Ill health, in any event, was too valuable a weapon to relinquish. Heroines in novels continued to contract smallpox, typhoid, tuberculosis and many mysterious and unnamed diseases that always necessitated cutting off their beautiful hair, which promptly grew back in masses of curls. There was no situation in a novel an attack of brain fever could not resolve, and determined young ladies even went so far as to die if they could prove their point in no other way. But the role of the confirmed invalid "enjoying ill health," the cheerful sufferer so common in the English domestic novels who spent a lifetime on the sofa, did not appeal to American women. They would be radiant, vigorous and active, fresh skinned, clear eyed, gay, daring and confident, perpetually young and always beautiful. It was in this new mold Mrs. Southworth cast her Capitola.

Thick clustering curls of jet black hair fell in tangled disorder around a broad white and smooth forehead, slender and quaintly arched black eyebrows placed about a pair of mischievous dark grey eyes that sparkled beneath the shade of long thick black lashes; a little turned up nose, and red pouting lips completed the character of a countenance full of fun, frolic, spirit and courage.

There had been "romps" in fiction before but Capitola added a new dimension to the role. Introduced to the reader disguised as a boy, in moments of stress she admonished herself: "Now, Cap, my little man, be a woman and don't stick at trifles." Spirited, beautiful, independent, unafraid, she flouted her guardian, "That look used to strike terror into the heart of the enemy. It doesn't into mine!" She fought a duel with a gentleman who slandered her and shot him full of dried peas; she outwitted Le Noir; she foiled the brigand Black Donald and his henchmen sent to kidnap her; she laughed at everyone including herself, thumbed her nose at her enemies, stuffed herself with tarts and "abhorred sentiment."

Her author loved Capitola:

How glad I am to get back to my little Cap; for I know very well, reader, just as well as if you had told me, that you have been grumbling for two weeks for the want of Cap. But I could not help it, for to tell the truth, I was pining after her myself which was the reason that I could not do half justice to the scenes of the Mexican war. Well now let us see what Cap has been doing—what oppressors she has punished—victims she has delivered—in a word, what new heroic adventures she has achieved.

Her guardian loved Capitola: "You deserve to have been a man, Cap. Indeed you do!"

Black Donald, the brigand chief, loved her, too. So did a million readers. The book joined Dickens' *A Tale of Two Cities*, George Eliot's *Adam Bede* and Thackeray's *The Virginians* on the best-seller list for 1859. Bonner published it twice again in the *Ledger*, in 1868 and 1883.

Not every woman, of course, was ready or able to be a Capitola. In the domestic novel and in real life the misunderstood, mistreated martyr still suffered and endured—and turned defeat into moral victory. But the frankness and humor, the assurance and independence of Capitola set a style that never went out of fashion.

At the conclusion of *The Hidden Hand*, Mrs. Southworth addressed a note to her readers:

Now, dear reader, my pleasant task is ended. Day and night have I wrought at it, cheered by your appreciation and by the goodness of the best publisher I have ever read. But my strength is not great nor my health good, and this week I go, with my two children, to recruit under the green shadows of Old English homes. And in leaving my native shore I feel like begging from you all, a kind "God bless you."

Soon after her arrival in England, Mrs. Southworth set to work again. To the *Ledger,* in weekly installments of twenty handwritten pages she sent: *The Doom of Deville, Rose Elmer,* and *Eudora,* and although their heroines lacked Capitola's magnetic charm, they found receptive audiences both at home and abroad.

In the absence of an international copyright agreement, Mrs. Southworth, strictly speaking, possessed no English serial "rights," but according to the custom of the time the London *Journal,* with Bonner's consent, acquired a moral title to her work—and an advantage over any competitors—by arranging to pay for her advance sheets for publication in their pages. Translations of her work also appeared on the Continent.

She enjoyed England—and accumulated a storehouse of "impressions" of the countryside and the customs that she drew on forever after. She made a wide circle of friends and through Mrs. Stowe became intimate with Lady Byron, but three years abroad were enough. In the spring of 1862, Mrs.

Southworth "so homesick I think my heart will break" came back to Prospect Cottage in Georgetown.

Trouble beset her almost immediately. Her new story, *Astrea,* got off to a bad start. "I'm sorry I didn't get the bride abducted soon enough for the first chapter," Mrs. Southworth apologized to Bonner. Subsequent installments arrived late at the *Ledger*'s offices—with the author's excuses. "I was two days in bed with a toothache—"; "I sent an Irish servant to the Post Office with the manuscript and she returned crazy with drink—enough to make one turn slave holder in self-defense." Bonner needed all his patience for the next news. Mrs. Southworth and her children had smallpox. Arrangements were made for someone to continue *Astrea.*

Despite this new threat to her life, Mrs. Southworth's general health had greatly improved during her years with the *Ledger.* Security, prestige, sympathy and understanding were the tonics her case required and Bonner supplied them. He wrote her frequently; he advised her about her children, her money and her book rights; he helped her needy relatives; he gave her a star's place on the *Ledger;* he promised to continue her salary if she were ill; he and his family exchanged visits with her; he sent her presents and large bonuses—without, however, increasing her basic weekly salary very much —for Bonner, like many men, was generous rather than just.

Mrs. Southworth, satisfied with her lot, never ceased asking Heaven "to reward and bless . . . the only benefactor I ever had in this world."

When Mrs. Southworth returned to the United States she was legally free to remarry—whether by Enoch Arden decree or the hand of God, she never made quite clear. Before her illness she had visitors from England and Bonner suspected one of them might be a prospective husband. One marriage was enough for Mrs. Southworth, however, and she assured her old friend that, while the man in question was "as near Christian perfection as any human could approach ... I will remain as I am, E. D. E. N. Southworth, and you will never lose your contributor."

Neither the altar nor the grave could sever her contract with Bonner. She made a rapid recovery from smallpox and was soon in such splendid health and spirits that when her carriage backed over a cliff and crashed to bits, "she got out undismayed and went home and had a jolly oyster roast." *Astrea* was finished and had "gained . . . by having new intellect infused into it," Mrs. Southworth generously declared.

Her thoughts turned to her next book which she described to Bonner as "one of the most beautiful love stories I ever imagined and if I can only have quiet and peace of mind and body I shall write it in a style that shall make some sensation."

She kept her promise and *Self-Made* (later published in two volumes as *Ishmael; or, In The Depths* and *Self-Raised; or, From the Depths*) became one of the ten best-selling books of the century. It was similar in many ways to Mrs. Southworth's other novels. There were five deserted wives and a fiendish villain with a villainess to match him; the full quota of long-lost relatives discovered each other; the usual abductions, mysterious disappearances, shipwrecks and runaway horses provided suspense. A large portion of the second volume was set in an English castle unusually well provided with trap doors, secret stairs, sliding panels and underground dungeons.

Although *Self-Made* had all the conventional trappings of her other books, the theme—the rags-to-riches rise of Ishmael from poverty to a position of honor—was new. Mrs. Southworth touched the heart of a people who believed in themselves and their country and she created a folk hero that, thanks to Alger, still survives.

If Capitola served as an ideal for the new woman, Ishmael was the model for the male. He was not only successful but "good." As an infant, before he could talk or walk, he crawled around the floor and helped his aunt by retrieving her thread, and he figuratively never rose from this position. He was obliging, docile and agreeable. He had blue eyes, fair hair, a pale, delicate complexion, an arch smile and he spoke in sweet, modulated tones. His illegitimacy and his lack of money further diminished his power.

When Ishmael educated himself and became a lawyer, as his first case he defended, without a fee, a deserted wife. As he pleaded for her in court "his face grew radiant as the face of an archangel." It seems obvious he shared another attribute of the heavenly beings, neuter gender. Where ladies were concerned he always knew his place—respectful, polite, devoted and quite contented to love from afar without hope of return. Mrs. Southworth in a preface to the book hoped "the youth of every land would take him for a Guiding Star."

10   Joy of Battle

In 1861 CIVIL WAR, so long threatened, finally came, changing the life and future of the nation and everyone in it. Like all wars, this one brought death and destruction, made widows, orphans and invalids, enriched and impoverished, freed and enslaved, and left the extra burden of guilt, fear and insecurity that internal conflicts invariably impose.

Little of this soul-shaking struggle or of the social, political and economic upheaval that followed appeared in the pages of the domestic novel although one, *Uncle Tom's Cabin*, many believed, had caused it all.

Abraham Lincoln was not entirely joking when at their first meeting he took Mrs. Stowe's hand in his and said, "So this is the little woman who made this big war."

Between *Uncle Tom's Cabin* and *Dred, A Tale of the Great Dismal Swamp*, a second and almost equally powerful novel showing slavery's effect upon free whites, Mrs. Stowe wrote a chatty, intimate, modest account of her triumphant tour of Europe in 1853. Neither this, nor in 1858 *Our Charley*, a practical guide to the management of small boys, differed very greatly from the pieces Mrs. Stowe had dashed off twenty years earlier to buy a new carpet or mattress or get out of one of the family's recurring financial "scrapes."

In 1862, with President Lincoln's approval and his assurance of an imminent Emancipation Proclamation, Mrs. Stowe answered the "Affectionate and Christian Address," from the women of England in 1853, with an appeal to their conscience and honor that did much to lessen the prevailing sympathy for the South and strengthen the Union cause in Great Britain. Thereafter, except for one later and ill-fated crusade, Mrs. Stowe made church, home and everyday life her chief literary interest. Her world and experience had enlarged; her understanding of people and their motives increased; her technique improved; but her novels, *The Minister's Wooing, The Pearl of Orr's Island, Agnes of Sorrento,* were quiet simple accounts reminiscent in mood, subject and content of her *Mayflower* tales. Through the bitterest days of the war, when Mrs. Stowe's heart was full of deep concern for her country and for her oldest son serving in the front lines, she wrote "Stories About our Dogs," "The Ravages of a Carpet," "Little Foxes, or the Insignificant Habits which Mar Domestic Happiness" and a series of articles on interior decoration published as *House and Home Papers.*

The other popular domestic novelists seemed equally disinterested. Even those who attacked or defended slavery most vigorously in the fifties remained silent.

Some were dead. Mrs. Hentz, while caring for her husband, contracted pneumonia and did not live to see *Ernest Linwood* published. Some lost their audience. Maria Cummins followed *The Lamplighter* with a rather similar tale of another indispensable woman, *Mabel Vaughn,* and that with *El Fureidis,* a story of Syria and Palestine written, the author said, "entirely from imagination." Neither enjoyed any great popularity nor did her last novel, *Haunted Hearts,* which appeared in 1864, two years before her death.

Some writers were busy. T. S. Arthur, who reached the peak of his popularity with *Ten Nights in a Barroom,* still turned out novels but his principal product was a series of state histories for the rapidly enlarging textbook market. Arthur's *Home Magazine,* however, supported the Union and the author graciously granted requests for his picture which invariably sold well at the Charity Fairs organized by the Sanitary Commission, forerunner of the Red Cross.

Mrs. Southworth, Maryland born and bred, had rather tolerated slavery in practice with her pictures of happy field hands and domineering mammies full of "comic talk," but she detested the institution in principle as she showed in the manumission theme of *India: The Pearl of Pearl River* in 1856. When war came, amid the pressures and conflicts of the Capital's divided society, she remained loyal to the Union and helped the wounded streaming north past her cottage in Georgetown and nursed many of them, including her daughter's fiancé, Lieutenant James V. Lawrence. Her son, despite Bonner's offer to buy him a substitute, joined the Army's Medical Corp and Mrs. Southworth rejoiced "when by the blessings of the Lord our successes in Pennsylvania are glorious" and felt, as she wrote Bonner, "my human nature rising above my education . . . when I saw she-rebels parading secession colors and openly proclaiming their sentiments. . . . There is nothing I hate on earth with a hatred so intense as I do a she-rebel."

In *Fair Play* and a sequel, *How He Won Her,* which followed *Ishmael,* Mrs. Southworth touched on the plight of the

Southerners who supported the Union. The story had four heroines—Britomarte, Alberta, Erminie and Elfie. The last-named, a lively young Virginian with something of Capitola's spirit, defied her secessionist neighbors, made a flag, hung it on the highest tree, dared the rebels to take it down and, true to her colors, shot the first man who tried. Then, as she later told her admiring Northern friends:

"I thought he was dead sure enough . . . lying with his head, arm and leg doubled under him. . . . I ran into the house and brought out a pitcher of water and a bottle of whiskey . . . dashed water in his face . . . opened his clenched teeth with an oyster knife . . . uncorked the bottle and poured the whiskey down his throat."

After a gun battle with the wounded man's supporters Elfie finally retreated to the Capital where she served her cause by trapping Confederate spies and encouraging her friend, Erminie, "who suffered, wept but remained steadfast to her principles, to refuse her Southern suitor. Britomarte, disguised, spent some time on the battlefields.

But these incidents filled only a small part of the two long volumes, and Mrs. Southworth devoted most of her attention to the adventures of Britomarte and her devoted admirer on a desert island chaperoned only by an Irish maid. In no later work did Mrs. Southworth ever mention the war again.

Marion Harland continued her precociously begun career with a second book, *The Hidden Path*, in 1855. The next year she married the Reverend Edward Payson Terhune and moved to Charlotte Courthouse, Virginia, where she wrote *Moss Side*. As dank in content as in title, the book told the story of Gracie barred from marrying Herbert because in the

distant past *his* father had seduced *her* aunt. After ten years
of vicissitudes and misunderstandings and fourteen deaths—
including that of Herbert's father—the couple were united.

Early in 1859 the Reverend Terhune accepted a call to
the First Reformed Church of Newark. During that year and
the next Marion Harland, journeying south on periodical
visits to her parents, saw, but like many others with unbeliev-
ing eyes, the mounting political tension.

She wrote in her autobiography:

> I am often asked if we were not uneasy . . . in the thick of
> sectional worldly strife. . . . The truth is I had been used to
> political wrangling from my youth up . . . so much that we heard
> was sheer gasconade amusing for a time from its very unreason
> and illogical conclusions and often indicative of such blatant
> ignorance of spirit and the resources of the Federal Government
> that I failed to attach to it the importance, the magnitude, the
> mischief deserved to have.

The Terhunes and their small children, in Richmond when
Virginia seceded, barely managed to catch the last through
train to the north. The ensuing four years were difficult ones
for Marion Harland. Her kinsmen, friends, and one brother
served in the Confederate Army. She loved Virginia; she understood and sympathized with the South, yet like her father
and her Northern husband, she believed in the principle of
the Union.

Grave personal cares came to the Terhunes. Marion Harland's younger sister, who lived with them, fell ill. They
managed to have her smuggled across the Potomac to Richmond only to hear of her death there from smallpox. Their
oldest child, at that time their only son, succumbed to

diphtheria. Added to all this, J. C. Derby, Marion Harland's publisher and old friend, unexpectedly failed in 1861. The royalties due her on *Nemesis,* a rather somber tale he published in 1860, were lost. During the war she published two collections of her earlier short stories and another novel, *Miriam,* that showed the author's heart and thoughts were preoccupied elsewhere.

At last the end came. Lee surrendered. Prisoners were exchanged, families reunited. "It was a divine breathing spell . . ." Marion Harland wrote in her autobiography, "for us and for the country—that summer of peace and plenty."

The Terhunes bought a country place in New Jersey and Marion Harland named it for a novel she had in progress, Sunnybank. (Nearly a half century later her second son, Albert Payson Terhune, on inheriting the property made it his kennel name and extended the title's literary life into the present with his tales of Lad and the other Sunnybank collies.)

The original *Sunnybank* took its name from the plantation of Morton and Ida Ross Lacey of *Alone* and continued the story of this couple and their grown children during the war years. It was a realistic, sane, conciliatory novel, well planned and well executed. The author told the story (and at the same time solved the difficult problem of presenting both Northern and Southern viewpoints) by alternating portions from the journal of Elinor Lacey in love with a Union officer and Agatha engaged to Elinor's brother in the Confederate Army. Elinor's father, like Marion Harland's, suffered a dual loyalty of conscience and between the raiders and the defenders a dual levy on his possessions and patience.

The plot for a novel of the period was rather simple. Elinor

139

promised to wait for Harry Wilton, her fiancé and a new-comer to Virginia, when he decided he must return north after secession. Agatha, a protégé of the family, although engaged to Elinor's brother, also loved Harry and schemed unsuccessfully to prevent his marriage to her rival. The contrasting characters of the girls were developed with real psychological insight. Elinor, the petted daughter of the house, good because she was happy, happy because she was loved, loved because she was good, began as a sentimental heroine but developed, under the stress of the war, into a woman of dignity and courage. In Agatha the author drew an excellent portrait of the girl without family, money or training who must live as a dependent in the house of friends, protected in theory from the harsh fate of working for wages but subjected, in reality, even under the best circumstances to a heavier task, eternal gratitude.

Early in the book Agatha writes in her diary:

If no one had ever treated me cruelly; if I had never looked vainly into a human face for love and smiles; if poverty, dependence, and enforced sycophancy were to me matters of far off hearsay, the probability is that I should be on excellent terms with myself and the world at large.

This clever, beautiful, spirited girl resented the attentions, kind words, and gifts of her benefactors and grew daily more embittered until finally she had to destroy either them or herself.

With more realism and justice and less sentimentality and heroics than many who have since approached the subject, Marion Harland described the four war years in a "fought over" corner of Virginia. She kept a scrupulous balance sheet: if Union troops raided, requisitioned and stole, so did Confederate soldiers. She showed men on both sides, fighting for what they honestly believed was a just cause, and the profiteers, opportunists and thieves, north and south, who laughed at them. She, almost alone among her contemporaries, dared to write that thousands died needlessly on the field, in the hospitals and in the prisons—equally dreadful above and below the Mason-Dixon line.

The book had the popularity it well deserved, but few of all the other domestic novelists did more than touch upon the theme.

The war they almost ignored had one important effect, however, upon the domestic novelists, indeed upon all writers. It created thousands of new readers. Not the slightest attempt was made to occupy the leisure of soldiers at the front, in camps or hospitals. Great masses of men away from home, alone, thrown on their own resources, had for recreation the brothel, the bottle, or the book. A surprising number became addicts of the latter.

Story papers, the *Ledger* and others, and the new cheap paper books went out by the thousands in bales and bundles to the army, where they were read, reread, passed from hand to hand, even traded across the lines.

In 1860 two brothers, Irwin and Erastus Beadle, like Robert Bonner, printers turned publisher, began issuing a series of popular books to sell at 10 cents. Cheap books had been tried before—during the publishers' war in the forties the price fell to 6¾ cents and Ballou of *The Flag of Our Union* published paper backs at 25 cents, but the Beadles succeeded where others failed although they made rather a strange choice for their first title, *Malaeska, The Indian Wife of the White Hunter* by Ann Stephens, a popular domestic novelist.

Born Ann Sophia Winterbotham in Connecticut in 1813, the author early displayed her literary gift, according to town gossip, by putting her criticisms and complaints about her neighbors into verses she dropped on their porches. At eighteen she married Edward Stephens, a journalist, and moved to Portland, Maine, where she took charge of two magazines established by her husband. In 1837 the Stephenses went to New York—he to work in the customhouse, she to edit the *Ladies' Companion*. Thereafter her name went from masthead to masthead—*Graham's, Peterson's, Brother Jonathan,* the *Ladies' World,* the *Illustrated Monthly,* the latter two, both short-lived, she established.

She knew almost everybody in the literary world. Touring Europe in 1850 she met Humboldt, Thackeray, and Dickens and, in turn, distinguished visitors to New York usually appeared at her literary salon. She was, to quote Mrs. Southworth, "large, fat, fair, light-haired, . . . blue-eyed and dressy," but this bisque doll visage hid a keen, clever mind. She was one of the few women published by T. B. Peterson who did not accuse him of ill treatment, impudence or fraud—perhaps because she mixed a kind of ponderous archness with business. "Shall I like the new partner?" she inquired in one of her letters to T. B. Peterson, "I mean, you know, just as much as is proper and genteel for an old married lady to do?"

Always a prodigious worker, in the decades before the

war, she wrote, besides her magazine pieces, two needlework guides, a tale of bucolic humor, *High Life in New York*, under the pseudonym Sam Slick, and seven novels, four of which were widely read.

The first two, *The Old Homestead* in 1854 and *Fashion and Famine* the next year, explored a scene rather new for the domestic novel—the rapidly growing city—a place of color and motion and variety, the hovels of the poor, the palaces of the rich, with tantalizing glimpses of the sin and vice and luxury urban life encouraged. As a contrast she pictured a countryside that existed only in retrospect— a place of fat cattle, full barns and well-stocked pantries. Beyond this Mrs. Stephens brought nothing new to the domestic novel—in general she improvised in the old themes. She described houses and furnishings, balls and costumes in lusher prose than Mrs. Hentz. In violence of action and complexity of plot she vied with Mrs. Southworth.

Malaeska, with which Beadle began his dime novel series, had appeared some years earlier in a woman's magazine. Malaeska, an Indian maiden, was sent by her dying husband, the white hunter, with their child to his proud parents in New York. They kept the child and, although they would not acknowledge a red-skinned daughter-in-law, allowed the mother to remain as a nurse. Malaeska tried to kidnap her child and, failing, returned to the woods. The boy grew up learning to hate Indians so much that when Malaeska disclosed her identity to him he committed suicide. Malaeska died the next day on the grave of her husband.

Malaeska deserves a place of honor as the noblest of the

many noble savages that glided through literature. Except for her name, her costume and her propensity for canoe travel she might have been any of the long-suffering wives in the domestic novel. She possessed all the requirements:

. . . a laugh as musical as birdsong, hair that glowed like raven wing and motion as graceful as an untamed gazelle . . . Her language was pure and elegant, sometimes even poetical beyond their comprehension. Her sentiments were correct in principle and full of simplicity. . . . She was never seen to be angry and a sweet patient smile always hovered about her lips . . . poetry of intellect and of warm deep feeling shed a loveliness over her face seldom witnessed on brow of savage.

She spent her life:

. . . in piling up soft couches for those she loved, and taking the cold stones for herself. It was her woman's destiny, not the more certain because of her savage origin. Civilization does not always reverse this mournful picture of womanly self-abnegation.

Beadle had another star contributor in Metta Victoria Fuller Victor the wife of his chief editor, Orville Victor. At fifteen already the author of several tales and poems, she wrote *The Last Days of Taul, a Romance of the Lost Cities of Yucatan* and followed this, rather ambitiously, with a sequel to *The Wandering Jew* for the *Home Journal*. Her temperance novel, *The Senator's Son*, in 1851 went into ten editions, over thirty thousand copies sold in England alone. In 1856 she married Orville Victor, a writer and journalist from Sandusky, Ohio, whom she met in New York. Shortly after her marriage the New York *Weekly* offered her a contract for $25,000 for five years for the exclusive rights to her serial stories for their pages. When her husband accepted the editorship of Beadle's Dime Library Mrs. Victor became his assistant and a frequent contributor.

Her fifth book for Beadle, issued in 1861, an antislavery novel, *Maum Guinea*, proved one of the Library's all-time best sellers, a favorite, it was said, of President Lincoln and, according to Henry Ward Beecher, extremely influential in counteracting Southern sentiment in England.

Mrs. Victor followed *Maum Guinea* with *The Unionist's Daughter* and many other novels under her own and a variety of pen names but none equaled the sales of these earlier titles.

Other women, too, wrote dime novels but not, if they wanted to sell them, in the sentimental pattern of *Malaeska* and *Maum Guinea*. For, just as women had a dream world and it was in the domestic novel, men, too, demanded one for themselves and found it in the "dime libraries" and "yellow backs," which very soon became a place where females scarcely existed and the best life was that of action, adventure, struggle and violence in a simple, single-sexed universe.

The story papers meantime came more and more to stress their "family" appeal, which meant stories for women readers. The *Ledger*, boasting Mrs. Southworth's "exclusive services," built circulation rapidly. Among Bonner's competitors who wanted their share of this profitable business was the New York *Weekly* founded by A. J. Williamson and purchased from him by Francis S. Street and Francis S. Smith, the latter a contributor, for $50,000 with a down payment of $100. The partners, if they were to pay off their debt, needed a writer to rival Mrs. Southworth and in 1859 they found one in Mrs. Mary Jane Holmes. Her first story for them, *Marian Grey*, is often credited with saving Street and

Smith from bankruptcy. Certainly this and other stories of hers helped increase the New York *Weekly*'s circulation from 28,000 to 100,000 in three years.

Mrs. Holmes, born in Massachusetts in 1825, a school-teacher at thirteen, began writing at an early age and published her first story at fifteen. At twenty-four she married Daniel Holmes, a young lawyer. Dan'l, as his wife called him, was frail and wisplike and subject to malarial attacks. In his later life ladies who lived along the way he followed from his home to the center of town provided chairs on their lawns so he might rest en route and he often had to be carried upstairs from the street to his office—not a very difficult task for he weighed less than a hundred pounds. He added dignity with a frock coat and stature with a top hat—for he was three years younger and several inches shorter than his famous wife.

Following their marriage the Holmeses spent a year in Versailles, Kentucky, then returned to New York State and in 1853 settled in Brockport, where Mr. Holmes practiced law and served as secretary of the Normal School and Mrs. Holmes began her first novel.

Appleton's, impressed by Putnam's success with *The Wide, Wide World*, published the book, *Tempest and Sunshine*, in 1854. From then on, Mrs. Holmes averaged almost a book a year until she died in 1907.

Tempest and Sunshine drew its title from the leading characters, two sisters, who like actors in a morality play justified their names by their appearance, personality and behavior. Tempest, a wicked brunette, hated her sister and by imitating her voice, forging her handwriting and similar de-

146

ceptions attempted to steal blonde Sunshine's suitor. She failed, received her just punishment, and Sunshine lived happily with her rich husband.

Mrs. Holmes's second book, *The English Orphans,* which Appleton's published in 1855, won readers and high praise on every side. The *North American Review*'s critics declared himself and a discriminating circle as "charmed." He continued:

The pathetic element stops short of mawkishness. The comic vein is worked with success. The characterization is exquisite. . . . The picture of rural and village life . . . deserve to be hung up in perpetual memory as types of humanity fast becoming extinct. . . . The dialogue is brief and pointed . . . and gracefully constructed. . . .

The English Orphans also told the story of two sisters— selfish Ella, the pet of a rich aunt who scorned poor noble Mary left on the town farm, until fate reverses their situation in life. This in general was the simple story Mrs. Holmes usually told.

The author, Mollie to her Dan'l, might have passed for any one of her own heroines. Described by her housekeeper, Mrs. Jennie Stewart, as:

slender, tall with a little stoop to hide it, curly hair and a false fringe she ordered by mail from Chicago, violet eyes, a sweet mouth . . . she loved everybody and everybody loved her. . . .

She taught Sunday school, built a parish house, tithed a tenth of her rapidly mounting income, organized a temperance society, a village reading room, a literary club and, during the depression of 1893, bread and soup kitchens for the unemployed. She opened her home to students of the local schools, helped the dependents of the Union soldiers during the war and the veterans themselves on their return, gave lectures, educated two Japanese girls she met on her travels, and dispensed cookies with a lavish hand to three generations of Brockport children.

Her housekeeper remembers:

There was nobody like her—when I was ill Mrs. Holmes nursed me and when I was well she let me wear her real seal skin coat to parties.

In life just as in her novels this goodness reaped rich rewards. Besides the "real seal skin," Mrs. Holmes had an ermine wrap, elegant clothes and handsome jewelry. When she finished her novel for the year and received the $4,000 to $6,000 the New York *Weekly* paid her for each one, she and her husband went traveling to England, Russia, California, France, the Orient and came home with crates of curios— a stone from Mars Hill, Egyptian candlesticks, a mosaic table, a Swiss music box, a piano cover embroidered by nuns, Savonarola's chair for the study and a totem pole for the front lawn.

After giving her first two books to Appleton's and several that followed to a local firm, Miller and Orton of Auburn who failed, Mrs. Holmes in 1863 took *Marian Grey* to G. W. Carleton, a piece of good fortune for both parties to the contract.

G. W. Carleton and his successor, J. W. Dillingham, knew the importance of the growing feminine audience and worked energetically to attract and keep authors who could please it.

Along with the royalty checks to Brown Cottage in Brockport went fruits for the table, flowers for the conservatory, new books and choice engravings. On one of his frequent visits to the Holmeses, Dillingham brought a massive silver tea set which he insinuated into the kitchen asking Mrs. Stewart, the housekeeper, to use it the following morning at breakfast. There, early at the table, the publisher, smiling, rubbing his hands with glee, enjoyed his favorite author's surprise and pleasure at the gift.

Mrs. Holmes's conception of the novel was more subtle than that of many of her contemporaries. She did not depend on Gothic horrors, violent action or exotic types. Her action was minimal, her characters commonplace, her plots repetitious, but her conflicts did arise out of a genuine difference in personality, culture, social or economic status.

She had two attributes almost lacking in the other domestic novelists—irony and humor. Flashes of both amid the cloying sweetness of her pages produce the same effect as pickles at a sugaring-off party in her native New England. She was curious and perceptive, an excellent reporter of the minutiae of everyday middle-class life, although she lacked not so much the intelligence as the education and experience to draw the fullest meaning from her observations. Her skill in reproducing the scene, the manners and customs of farm and village with fidelity and color gave her work a certain realism. Consciously, or not, she wrote the novel of manners. If she did not achieve great artistic success with the form, neither did she completely fail.

Following Mrs. Hentz's plan for managing the male, Mrs.

Holmes evolved several new methods of curtailing his power. In *Darkness and Daylight* she made one man blind and the other guilt-ridden because he concealed an insane wife. In both *The English Orphans* and *Meadowbrook* the crime was minor—fortune hunting or philandering. A few were wounded or caught "slow fever" on the battlefield—others lacked education or the social graces.

The earlier domestic novelists had usually depicted the struggle of life as woman against man. For Mrs. Holmes it was usually woman against woman, rival against rival, youth against age, sister against sister, a meeting of opponents truly worthy and equal. The male, impaired physically, mentally, morally, no longer a protagonist, came to be a trophy, a token prize for the victor.

Why, it might be inquired, did none of these women ever consider divorce as an escape from the troublesome creatures who plagued their lives? In theory at least the way was open to them. Marriage in colonial America was considered a civil contract that might be terminated by the same authority that sanctioned it, and although some states made the severance difficult and expensive, others (Indiana, in particular, where Robert Owen's idealistic dreams of sex equality influenced the state statutes) enjoyed a reputation as "divorce colonies." Economically, it was also feasible as long as the needs of an agrarian pioneer society made a woman, especially one with children, a valuable asset for any man.

Yet relatively few women took advantage of the situation for there were strong deterrents. The church frowned upon divorce, some denominations more severely than others, but all issued periodic warnings against it. Several notorious cases, such as that of Fanny Kemble Butler *vs*. Pierce Butler, served to warn women that, wherever else their influence prevailed, the courts, still a bulwark of masculine privilege, were apt to deal harshly with women who questioned their husbands' judgment or authority.

As the fallen woman in earlier society had become an object of contempt and distrust for the simple economic reason that she threw away a valuable commodity, so did suspicion now fall upon the women reckless enough to risk her position, her possessions and the custody of her children in a divorce court.

Consequently none of the domestic novelists except T. S. Arthur in a tract or two ever treated the subject until well after the Civil War.

In the seventies, following a series of well-publicized "divorce mill" scandals and a nationwide movement for better enforcement of stricter laws, Mrs. Holmes used the theme in her *Daisy Thornton* in 1878. The misunderstandings of Daisy, a child bride of fifteen, and her husband were magnified by her scheming father, who persuaded her to a divorce.

The husband married again but Mrs. Holmes's argument was that first wives, as long as they live, have certain inalienable rights that can never be changed—not by man or law or custom or accident. Even the second wife in *Daisy Thornton* agreed with this premise. She was kind and understanding, and self-effacing. She named her child after her predecessor and finally, as one who knew her place, died of smallpox so the marriage of her husband and his first wife could be resumed.

Any struggle between man and woman had to be resolved, it seemed, on home ground—under the old rules—with the original players. Divorce was no solution. Changing husbands did not change men or the society that made them. Or possibly women had grown such skilled campaigners in the struggle of the sexes that they took more joy in the battle itself than in the prospect of eventual victory.

11 ❧ Choice of Weapons

THE SOUTH, both before and during the war, had its share of "fair patriots" who blasted away at the North but their sentiments, sufficiently impassioned to sustain the verse, essay or sketch, ofttimes faltered at longer forms and the few who did try the novel made no more literary capital out of the war than did their Yankee contemporaries.

It was not lack of firsthand material—no one bore a heavier burden than Southern women: four long years of death, destruction, privation and humiliation only the invaded and defeated know.

Basically, war has little real interest for normal women. It arises from man's mistake; its pursuit threatens the two major products of feminine creativity, human beings and homes; its effect, by reducing the male population, produces an unfavorable sex ratio.

Yet despite this the question of abolishing war itself never occurred to any of the domestic novelists. All, with the exception of Marion Harland, saw greater evils in boarding out, putting brandy in a pudding, or dancing the polka on Sunday than in mass slaughter.

Chief defender of the Confederacy among the domestic

novelists was Miss Augusta Jane Evans, who began her career at seventeen by writing a novel as a Christmas gift for her father. By birth and background the young author had entré to the best society of the South for her mother, Sarah, was "a Howard" and Augusta Jane, born in Columbus, Georgia, in 1835, "looked a Howard." Unfortunately before she could exercise her right to join the charmed circle of belles, her father, Matt Evans, through mismanagement or misplaced trust, failed in business and eventually lost his capital, his wife's wedding portion and their home. Like scores of other dispossessed Southerners, Mr. Evans took his family and moved west to recoup his fortunes in the promised land of Texas.

There Augusta Jane Evans wrote *Inez, A Tale of the Alamo*. When the Texas venture proved unprofitable and the family returned to Columbus, Mr. Evans enlisted the aid of a prosperous relative who arranged for Harper's to publish the book in 1855.

The limited sale did nothing to improve the fortunes of the Evans family. They occupied a cottage on the estate of relatives and Augusta Jane "visited around" earning local fame and occasional pin money writing book reviews while she worked on another novel, *Beulah*. This, when submitted, evoked so little interest at Harper's that the manuscript was mislaid. Miss Evans, accompanied by the necessary "male escort," a cousin, came to New York and after threatening suit recovered the precious parcel and went to Appleton's, only to meet another refusal. The young cousin, incensed by this unchivalrous reception, determined to throw the manuscript at the head of any future publisher who said no

. . . a fate J. C. Derby whom Miss Evans tried next fortunately escaped. Impressed, as he wrote later, by "the pleasant address and marked intelligence" of his caller, he took her book home and, like Mr. Putnam, gave it to his family to read. "The verdict was unanimous as to its merit."

Beulah, published in 1859, received generally favorable notices, although one critic did complain it was stolen from *Bleak House.* Miss Evans indignantly denied she had ever read that work and a comparison of the books makes it doubtful if the critic had either. Mr. Derby sold 22,000 copies of *Beulah* before the year ended.

Augusta Evans had just started her third novel, *Macaria,* when Georgia seceded and the author plunged into war work. The Beulah Guards, a home defense unit, and Camp Beulah were both named in her honor. At the latter, a small hospital near her home, she soothed fevered brows, wrote letters, distributed broth and jelly, acting, one admirer declared, as "a typical guardian angel." Less popular ladies charged that Miss Evans spent more time dancing with the officers than washing the enlisted men's feet, but she proved her devotion to the cause by giving *Macaria,* dedicated "to the brave soldiers of the Southern Army," to West and Johnson of Richmond who published the volume on brown wrapping paper, a prophetic symbol in that year of 1864 of the failure to compete with the North in manufacturing that ultimately brought about the Confederacy's defeat.

Less than the last third of the volume touched on the war, but in that portion Miss Evans spoke some harsh words about Yankees—demagogues, despots, hypocrites full of cant, "mischievous element of New England Puritanism." Her public opinion, however, did not altogether coincide with her private practices. By blockade runner via Cuba she sent a copy of *Macaria* to Mr. Derby. While making arrangements for a Northern edition under J. B. Lippincott's imprint, Derby discovered that a Michael Doolady, who earlier obtained a copy of *Macaria*, had a pirated edition of 5,000 copies ready for binding.

Derby, zealous in behalf of his rebel protégé, persuaded Lippincott to relinquish his rights and join him in forcing Doolady to pay a royalty to them in trust for Miss Evans. Northern readers, equally magnanimous, overlooked the slurs on their president, their regional institutions, and their character and bought enough copies of the book so that when shortly after Lee's surrender Miss Evans and her "male escort," this time a younger brother, appeared in J. C. Derby's office some good news awaited her.

As Mr. Derby described the scene:

noticing her attire, I suggested that a new dress and a new bonnet would not be out of place. . . . She said, "Mr. Derby, my father has lost everything . . . I have no money with which to replenish my wardrobe." I then told her for the first time that she had a considerable amount subject to her order, for copyright received on Macaria.

With these funds to support her Miss Evans set to work on another novel. In 1866 her *St. Elmo* won an audience that places it securely among the ten most popular novels ever published in the United States.

The book made an immediate and enormous impact upon the whole country—plantations, steamboats, coaches, schools, hotels, a variety of merchandise, a punch, a cigar, thirteen

American towns and an uncounted number of boys, sons of romantic mothers, bore the magic title.

The popularity was well founded, for in this and her earlier books Augusta Jane Evans not only included and elaborated upon every tactical theme that had hitherto appeared in the domestic novel but she introduced some new techniques.

Her books had, first of all, that dependable similarity in plot, setting and incident which readers of the domestic novel found so comfortable. Like Susan Warner and Maria Cummins and so many others, her favorite character was a poor, orphaned girl.

Miss Evans herself, none could deny, was a most devoted daughter. With the fortune her books earned "she accomplished the darling desire of her heart," she confided to a contemporary biographer, "to free her father from the burdens of care and financial embarrassment." She testified frequently to her mother's "wonderful clearness of judgment, the breadth and richness of her intellectual resources, her unswerving loyalty to duty and the purity and nobility of her lofty standards."

But in her novels parents represented surplus equipment to be removed as early as possible from the scene. Those who lingered did so only to be defied by their offspring.

Miss Evans' composite heroine, in early adolescence, usually entered the home of a benefactor. Provided with food, clothing, many social and every educational advantage, this brilliant, talented, stubborn girl is by any standard remarkably well treated, indeed indulged.

But dependency even under the best conditions, as Marion

Harland demonstrated in *Sunnybank,* corrodes character. The insecurity of her role, more than servant, less than daughter, always made the girl bitter, moody, unduly sensitive, frequently ill-tempered, and always fiercely ambitious and aggressively independent (the very soul sister in fact of all the women, young and old, who with or without cause considered themselves misunderstood, mistreated, misjudged).

Unlike Ellen and Fleda and Gerty, Augusta Jane Evans' young ladies wasted neither tears nor tact on their plight. Each resolved not only to escape her anomalous, humiliating position but to do so through her own unaided efforts. Her goal—a career in one of the few fields open to women, teaching, singing, writing, painting; her method of achieving it—unremitting application. To this end she studied and practiced and read books; she memorized pages and accumulated facts; she acquired skills, scarcely stopping to eat or sleep until, as a kind of unofficial graduation ceremony, she succumbed to brain fever.

In the first paragraphs of her first novel, *Inez,* Augusta Jane Evans set the tone for much that came after:

"There is the bell for prayers, Florry; are you ready?" said Mary Irving hastily entering her cousin's room. . . .
"Yes, I rose earlier than usual this morning, have solved two problems, and translated nearly half a page of Telemaque."
"I congratulate you on your increased industry and application. . . . I do wish, dear Florry, you could imbue me with some of your fondness for metaphysics, and mathematics," Mary replied with a sigh.

For the next thirty years a succession of Florrys did their best to oblige. Physics and metaphysics, mathematics and mythology, Greek, Hebrew, astronomy, no subject was too abstruse, no ancient papyrus too esoteric for Miss Evans' heroines.

Some critics found these attempts at self-improvement ridiculous: Edna Earl, anxious to acquire "a smattering of Chaldee"; Beulah, sitting over her books until three every morning; Irene Huntington, peering into her telescope all through the night; Salome Owen singing scales on the lonely shore—all provided a rich and inexhaustible source of humor in some circles. The author came in for her share of ridicule, for taking her own advice and emulating her own heroines she stuffed her pages with so many aphorisms, quotations, symbols, parables, similes and metaphors that to bring home a cow from pasture required a dozen classical allusions. *St. Twel'mo*, a parody by Charles Webb which appeared the year after *St. Elmo*, declared that its author while teething on a dictionary had inadvertently swallowed the volume.

The humorists overlooked some serious and important facts. Women were discovering that they, just as well as men, could acquire higher education and the inherent power it conferred. The untiring efforts of Emma Willard and her sister, Mrs. Almira Phelps, Mary Lyon and many other brave and now forgotten pioneers were opening the doors of colleges and universities to women who in the years following the war quickly took advantage of their opportunity.

Miss Evans was not the only writer who recognized this new trend. Some of Mrs. Southworth's heroines began to go to boarding school and Mary J. Holmes saw that hers received enough training to enable them to earn a living as teachers. Marion Harland's young ladies read and studied

159

with more enthusiasm than they attended parties.

Higher education, familiarity with the work of Darwin and Huxley, research into paleontology and geology which shook the religious beliefs of some students only strengthened the faith of women, at least in the domestic novel, and gave them a tighter hold on the keys to the kingdom.

Miss Evans' first book, *Inez, A Tale of the Alamo,* was the customary religious tract all apprentices of the domestic novel seemed bound to produce—but with these differences. Mary, the central figure in *Inez,* concerned herself not only with broad questions of spiritual belief but with the more specialized problems of denominational practice as she struggled to keep her aunt, uncle, cousin and several minor characters from accepting Catholicism. Her methods, too, were new. Ellen, Fleda, Gerty, the earlier heroines, ignored or transcended any knotty points of doctrine or history and relied on a teardrop, a text, a sunset "to further the Kingdom." But with all the vehemence and documentation of a state's attorney Mary presented so many facts, figures, comparative versions of the Gospels, writings of the early Church Fathers and references to ancient records that she bested the Jesuit priest in every argument, nullified his conversions and garnered several recruits of her own.

With the exception of the Catholic journals, no one objected to the intolerance and prejudice in *Inez.* The social climate favored such a viewpoint.

In the East the rising tide of Irish immigration, in the Southwest the desperate need for Texas in the program of national expansion, fostered an anti-Catholic sentiment which as early as 1836 took literary form in *The Awful Disclosures of Maria Monk* and later found political expression in the rise of the Know-Nothing party.

Older and wiser observers than Miss Evans justified the war with Mexico on the grounds that "wily Jesuits" spearheading Catholic power were determined not only to keep but eventually increase their territory and authority.

After Augusta Evans the denominational pattern, though usually unnamed, was sharply defined. Catholics were suspect although the superstitious ignorance of the Irish sometimes offered comic relief; Quakers tended to be at best eccentric, at worst hypocrites; Mormons, lascivious; Episcopalians, haughty and proud, with a touch of the whited sepulcher—in the domestic novel the ideal communicant belonged to one of the democratic although well-organized Protestant churches with a simple ritual and a strict discipline pastored by a beautiful and benign old saint or a noble and handsome young idealist who recognized the spiritual superiority of woman.

Miss Evans devoted her second novel entirely to the problem that sometimes arose with higher education—the loss of faith that led to skepticism, to agnosticism, even atheism. Her Beulah lived through this dreadful trial. She doubted, questioned, searched, fainted and fell before, in the concluding chapters, she emerged victorious, able to reconcile all human knowledge with fundamental theology.

Like Marion Harland, Miss Evans, too, had the satisfaction of knowing her books saved souls. Two men, reclaimed from vice and infidelity, wrote that they offered prayers for her at their family altars.

The heroes, if so they may be called, of Augusta Evans' first three novels were shadowy creatures barred by varied handicaps from making any serious sexual demands upon women—one was too old and an atheist; another, too genteel; a third, too poor and, almost as bad, the son of a murderer. The only "normal" display of masculine interest in the opposite sex became "abnormal" since the man involved, the Jesuit priest in *Inez*, broke his holy vows in declaring his passion.

The consummated marriage had little literary interest for Miss Evans. In *Inez* three of the four principals die—one young lady of tuberculosis, another of a broken heart, the object of their mutual affections by a Mexican bullet. Indeed, the whole novel was little better than a shambles—one hundred and fifty-eight men fell at the Alamo, four hundred at Goliad, a whole town succumbed to cholera, parents, relatives and friends expired from assorted causes until scarcely a page lacked "a stiffening corpse."

Beulah, in Miss Evans' second novel, finally married her guardian but only "when his locks are white." In *Macaria* two ladies who loved the same man reconciled themselves to his death in battle by opening a School of Design where "the primary branches of art should be popularized and thrown open to the masses."

The equanimity of these young ladies was understandable —such men while alive offered little challenge; when dead, few regrets.

St. Elmo Murray, the hero of Miss Evans' fourth book, was a moral cripple; an atheist; a murderer, for he had killed a man in a duel; a seducer with one of his victims dead of a broken heart and another in a convent, but nonetheless a man—virile, violent, rich, mysterious, domineering, sardonic, menacing, handsome. Therein lay the book's appeal—a worthy opponent and a real struggle for sex superiority.

Edna Earl's first glimpse of St. Elmo

filled her with instantaneous repugnance; there was an innate and powerful repulsion which she could not analyze. He was a tall, athletic man, not exactly young . . . and, though not one white thread silvered his thick, waving, brown hair, the heavy and habitual scowl on his high full brow had plowed deep furrows such as age claims for its monogram. His features were bold, but very regular; the piercing, steel-gray eyes were unusually large, and beautifully shaded with long, heavy, black lashes, but repelled by their cynical glare and the finely-formed mouth, which might have imparted a wonderful charm to the countenance, wore a chronic, savage sneer, as if it only opened to utter jeers and curses. Evidently the face had once been singularly handsome, in the dawn of his earthly career, when his mother's good-night kiss rested like a blessing on his smooth, boyish forehead and the prayer learned in the nursery still crept across his pure lips; but now the fair chiseled lineaments were blotted by dissipation, and blackened and distorted by the baleful fires of a fierce, passionate nature, and a restless, powerful, and unhallowed intellect. Symmetrical and grand as that temple of Juno, in shrouded Pompeii, whose polished shafts gleamed centuries ago in the morning sunshine of a day of woe, whose untimely night has endured for nineteen hundred years; so, in the glorious flush of his youth, this man had stood facing a noble and possibly a sanctified future; but the ungovernable flames of sin had reduced him, like that darkened and desecrated fane, to a melancholy mass of ashy arches and blackened columns, where ministering priests, all holy aspirations, slumbered in the dust.

163

All the Happy Endings

Poor, friendless Edna Earl, dependent on St. Elmo's charity and his mother's good will for her home, what weapons did she possess to use against this devastating male?

She was courageous and beautiful.

The large black eyes held a singular fascination in their mild sparkling depths, now full of tender loving light and childish gladness; and the flexible red lips curled in lines of orthodox Greek perfection, showing remarkable versatility of expression; while the broad, full, polished forehead with its prominent, swelling brows, could not fail to recall, to even casual observers, the calm, powerful face of Lorenzo de' Medicis, which, if once looked on, fastens itself upon heart and brain, to be forgotten no more.

She had read and memorized enough so that she could trade quotations and match metaphors on terms of equality with St. Elmo. Most of all, she possessed an inner conviction of righteousness, an unshakable faith in herself as an instrument of God.

Eventually St. Elmo, jilted in his youth and scornful of all women, succumbed to Edna Earl's charm.

A tinge of red leaped into his cheek, something that would have been called hope in any other man's eyes looked out shyly from under his heavy black lashes, and a tremor shook off the sneering curl of his bloodless lips.

Drawing her so close to him that his hair touched her forehead, he whispered;

"If I believe in you, my . . . it is in defiance of judgement, will, and experience, and some day you will make me pay a most humiliating penalty for my momentary weakness. Tonight I trust you as implicitly as Samson did the smooth-lipped Delilah;

164

tomorrow I shall realize that, like him, I richly deserve to be shorn for my silly credulity."

It was not an easy conquest. St. Elmo tempted Edna to pry into his sanctuary, to lie, to doubt her God, even to love him as he was. Edna Earl, incorruptible and immovable, would have him on her own terms—or not at all.

St. Elmo resisted as long as possible but his determination and self-control did not equal Edna Earl's. Not until he repented his youthful heresy, made what restitution he could for his crimes and became a minister was he allowed "to put his hand under her chin, draw the lips to him and kiss her repeatedly."

The "loveless marriage" was a relationship conceived and idealized by the domestic novelists. This was not the marriage of convenience known to Europeans, or the family-arranged marriage of Asiatic cultures, alliances where two people for social, financial or family reasons and without any pretense of romantic love made a working partnership. The loveless marraige in the domestic novel was something quite different. Here, in the true sentimental tradition, the man loved— madly, passionately, fiercely, threateningly. The woman did not, yet through a series of circumstances, developed with infinite variations by the novelists—to protect her father's fortune, her brother's honor, her mother's secret—the unwilling bride went to the altar.

Almost all of the domestic novelists depicted some form of this unhappy relationship—Mrs. Southworth had her fifteen-year-olds married to graybeards, Mrs. Holmes specialized in the worldly woman who married for position or wealth but carried a cherished memory of an earlier, dearer love whom she unfailingly recollected whenever church bells rang or hymns were played at twilight. Marion Harland used the theme in several books and devoted one entire novel to it, *At Last,* published in 1870.

Mabel Aylett, jilted by her fiancé, accepted the proposal of another man saying:

"I believe you to be a good true man and that the attachment you profess for me is sincere. I believe, moreover, that my chances of securing real peace of mind will be fairer, should I commit myself to your guardianship, that if I were to surrender my affections to the keeping of one whose vows were more impassioned, who, professing to adore me as a divinity, should yet be destitute of your high moral principle and stainless honor . . . I will not deceive you into the persuasion that I can ever feel for you, or any other man, the love, or what I thought was love, I knew in the few brief weeks of my early betrothal. . . . If friendship—if esteem, and the resolve to show myself a worthy recipient of your generous confidence—will content you, all else shall be as you wish."

Mabel was singularly unfortunate in the kind of men she attracted. Her husband proved "hard as flint," but her cool superiority carried her through the volume until the point where her first love was widowed. Providentially about the same time she discovered her husband had a "hereditary propensity to softening of the brain" which he had carefully concealed from her.

She had never been so near loving him as at the instant in which he believed he had incurred her everlasting displeasure. Generosity and pity were fast undoing the petrifying influences of her early disappointment, their mutual reserve and tacit misunderstandings.

166

Fortunately, he died a few pages later and left Mabel free to marry her early suitor.

The loveless marriage long since became part of our folklore and we are conditioned to feel sympathy for the poor girl coerced, persuaded or bartered into the horror of such a relationship—forgetting meantime that the real victim was perhaps the husband forced eventually, unless he could redeem the conventional pledge, "I shall teach you to love me," to choose between infidelity or impotence.

All of Miss Evans' early books had offered some example of the danger women ran in displaying their love. Inez, Electra in *Macaria*, Beulah, Edna in *St. Elmo*, all paid a bitter price for indulging in this weakness.

The ice maidens were the ones who always commanded devotion. If they were not actually dying, like Mary in *Inez*, "wasted, yet beautiful," they gave that impression. Beulah, pale and wan, her lips rigid and her hands cold, dressed in spotless white. Irene in *Macaria*, sending her lover to war, "endured his long searching gaze like another Niobe . . . there was no quiver in the icy white fingers."

Around this theme Miss Evans built all of her next book, *Vashti*, published two years after *St. Elmo*. The ever-present orphan girl, Salome Owen, fell in love with her benefactor's brother. Her devotion, expressed in "a strange, almost ferocious expression," "dilated nostrils," "burning glances," "half-smothered cries," only repelled Ulpian Grey. He preferred Agla Gerome, a recluse—with "snowy fingers," "steely eyes," "white hair," "a chill face," "a bluish pallor around the mouth," "delicate nostrils, almost transparent in their waxen curves," "a beautiful pale priestess consecrated to the shrine of sorrow." She wore blue, explaining with a sigh, "it is considered a mortuary color." She played sad music and read sad poetry and painted sad pictures as she gradually faded away.

When Dr. Grey noted that "the ivory flesh was shrinking closer to the small bones . . . the diaphanous hands were so thin that the sapphire asp glided almost off the slender finger," he proposed.

Probably few flesh-and-blood men shared Dr. Grey's necrolatry but many must have learned—and to their sorrow too late—what they accepted as maidenly reserve was instead militant frigidity, doubly vicious because it arose not from apathy or ignorance but from anger and revenge.

12 ✣ The Innocent
Bystander

In 1852, EMBOLDENED by the success of *The Wide, Wide World,* Susan Warner asked Mr. Putnam if he would advise her to write for a living or make shirts.

He replied rather cautiously, "I should not dare to offer even suggestions touching the difference between pens and needles—but it is fair to say that many have chosen the pen with less warrant and encouragement."

Many certainly had. Soon Susan Warner's younger sister, Anna, by far the kinder and prettier of the pair, began a literary career of her own under the name Amy Lothrop. Her *Dollars and Cents* in 1852 and *My Brother's Keeper* in 1855 sold well enough to continue in print after the war.

Susan Warner followed *Queechy* with twenty novels— all had the piety and moralizing but none of the charm of her first two. The women in them were, perhaps, too meek and the men too masterful to suit the taste of readers who had known Capitola and seen Edna Earl conquer St. Elmo. The sales were small.

Several juveniles and a collection of tales in five volumes called *Ellen Montgomery's Book-Shelf* in which the sisters collaborated proved slightly more popular.

All the Happy Endings

Despite their hard work, the Warners never achieved any real financial security. To cover their father's obligations, his support and their own, the litigation and upkeep on their island home, they sold profitable titles outright for small sums in ready cash. They wrote books they did not like; they corrected examination papers for teachers; they prepared Bible lesson outlines, Sunday-school guides, and attempted, unsuccessfully, a juvenile magazine.

Susan was satisfied. She adored her father. "She had only one Shrine of perfection and it was for him," Anna wrote in her biography. When still more money was needed, the sisters raised vegetables and sold them on the mainland.

The popularity of *The Wide, Wide World* and *Queechy* continued. As a kind of a badge of respectability and a salute to the Master, later authors from Louisa May Alcott to Kathleen Norris let *their* heroines read the two books. Sunday-school libraries were filled with stories of dedicated girls who found and converted atheists with the same zeal that the boys in the dime novels shot and skinned buffaloes.

Most popular of all Susan Warner's imitators was Miss Martha Finley, who wrote what came to be familiarly known as "the Elsie books" at the rate of nearly one a year from 1867 until 1909. The series was admired and condemned, revered and ridiculed, recommended and rejected by the most eminent authorities and, more important, read by millions. With the exception of Mark Twain's Huckleberry Finn, Elsie Dinsmore is probably the best known character ever to appear in American fiction.

The sex pattern of the period is well indicated in the contrast of the characters. Huck was anarchistic, his wickedness overt, almost conventional. In Elsie Dinsmore, however, under a cloak of pious prudery the most unwholesome relationships and suspect behavior were developed in an atmosphere of vulgar snobbery.

Almost any American woman over forty can recall the Elsie books and tell their story: "Elsie was awfully good and her father made her play the piano or else wouldn't let her play the piano and Elsie sat on the piano stool until she fainted and fell on the floor and cracked her head open or got brain fever or something and *then* her father felt awful." This in effect was the theme of the entire series.

Elsie, seven when the story began, lived with a stern grandfather, a cruel step-grandmother and an indifferent family of young uncles and aunts on a plantation. Her young father had been absent most of her life blaming her for her mother's death. Thanks to her Scotch nurse and later a devoted Negro servant, Chloe, Elsie was extremely religious and when her father finally returned she did her best to win his love and make him a Christian. The piano episode came in the middle of the first book when Mr. Dinsmore commanded Elsie to play for his friends on a Sunday and, since this violated her beliefs, she sat at the piano until she fainted, striking her head as she fell. Her father's repentance and grief was abject enough to please the most demanding.

Another clash of wills from which Elsie again emerged victorious occurred in the second volume. Thereafter Mr. Dinsmore's adoration and protection of his daughter assumed rather questionable intensity. He "fondled her hair," he "pressed her lips again and again to his," he "folded her to his heart"; he "drew her to his knees" and kept her there hour after hour; he declared at least every other chapter, "You belong to me." "You are *mine*, all mine, only mine!" Elsie was subjected to an ever-increasing list of taboos—some so arbitrarily evolved they seemed almost ceremonial in character. She was forbidden to eat hot breads, sit on the floor, read fiction (except *The Wide, Wide World*), wear combs in her hair or use a sewing machine more than a half hour.

If, like all Vestal Virgins, Elsie paid a high price for her power and ascendancy, she seemed content. She held the Keys to Heaven; she led her father to its gates; she had his complete attention.

Martha Finley, Elsie's creator, was born in 1828 in Chillicothe, Ohio, where her father practiced medicine. Dr. Finley became a controversial figure in a local dissension and moved on to South Bend, Indiana. The family were stanch Presbyterians and Martha Finley taught a Sunday-school class. After her mother's death, her father remarried and soon had a new family and Martha Finley went to relatives in the East. She taught school and tried her hand at some moral tales which she sent to the Presbyterian Publication Board. All the large denominations supported similar organizations well staffed with dependable writers who could turn out material for the Sunday-school libraries, a large and an important market.

Martha Finley's first efforts were so well received that she soon devoted her full time to the field and between 1856 and 1866 wrote twenty-five short tales, a great many modeled on Miss Warner's early books. Mysie in *Mysie's Work* was another Fleda who put her uncle's household to rights. Lily in *A Day in Lily's Life*, who was Ellen Montgomery grown richer and more angelic, eventually became, through another transmigration, Elsie Dinsmore.

During the war Martha Finley suffered a severe back injury and, unable to work, in pain and dependent on her half brother, she prayed for a miracle. The idea for *Elsie Dinsmore* she felt was her answer. She worked three and a half years on the book and then went to Dodd, Mead, who liked the story and decided to publish it as two separate volumes, one in 1867 and the other the following year.

Elsie's real popularity did not begin until 1869. From then on she was a fixture in American literature. The two original volumes grew to six, the usual number most series then contained, and Miss Finley began "the Mildred books," the story of Elsie's cousin, but readers demanded more of Elsie herself.

There was remarkably little to tell. Having converted her father, Elsie extended her benign influence to all other sinners with the possible exception of Catholics and Mormons. She devoted a volume apiece to exposing the faulty doctrines of these sects. She eventually married her father's oldest friend, Mr. Travilla, who remained in the story until seven children had appeared, by a kind of literary parthenogenesis. Augusta Evans Wilson's heroines were frigid. Elsie was asexual. Once sufficient children were on hand Mr. Travilla was killed—a necessity Martha Finley deplored but said her publishers demanded. Elsie, basking in her father's devotion, survived her widowhood.

Martha Finley had never been below the Mason-Dixon line when she began her famous series and consequently she was not hampered by any factual considerations in describing life on the various estates which Elsie, who was as rich as she was good, owned in various parts of the South.

As early as Defoe's *Moll Flanders* the plantation possessed a peculiar interest for women readers and this intensified after the Civil War. Supposedly when Lee surrendered the Old South died. With the mansions destroyed by Sherman and his brothers-in-arms, the brave men buried at Gettysburg, Chancellorsville and the Wilderness, the beautiful women reduced to abject poverty, the happy slaves made surly by freedom, the grace and charm of a leisurely world vanished.

But almost immediately a new South was born. Writers, painters, musicians, returning soldiers, romanticists, and unreconstructed rebels created and perpetuated an antebellum Dixie that never existed, but which, nevertheless, satisfied some general needs. There was the Negro, as valuable for his psychic contribution as for his physical labor. He was loyal and devoted to his master, whose worth inspired it; he was lazy and stupid to point up the white man's ambition and intelligence; paradoxically, he was also a source of folk wisdom and native shrewdness—a reassuring proof of nature's equalizing mercy in supplying deficiencies.

The master, courtly, chivalrous, handsome, served a purpose, too. As only the free-born republican can, Americans delighted in the aristocrat, to observe his appearance, his behavior, his accouterments, his habitat. Now they had a native species to keep as a kind of exotic pet; the dangerous nature of the creature when allowed full freedom only added to his charm.

Most important of all, especially for the readers of the domestic novel, was the belle—her curls cascading over her shoulders, her hoops swaying, her voice fluting, her power and influence unobtrusive but supreme, she was what every woman longed to be. Whether, as in the more secular tales of Mrs. Southworth and Mrs. Holmes, she sang and waltzed and flirted, or whether, like little Eva and little Elsie, she sang and prayed and distributed calf's foot jelly to the needy, she was always good, beautiful and happy, adored and protected by family, friends and servants.

The plantation symbol served another purpose for readers of the domestic novel. It was a panacea to cure a chronic affliction—homesickness. The population of the United States was on the move. (By 1850 one-third of the people born in Virginia, North and South Carolina and Georgia lived outside the state of their birth. New Englanders were equally footloose.) Men found a certain adventure in life in the frontier, the West, the lonely outposts, the scattered clearings. Women did not. For them it meant monotony and discomfort, pain and terror. Under the greatest difficulties they cared for their families, cooked, washed, sewed, bore and nursed and taught their children. Miles from other families, denied the release men found in drinking, hunting, gambling, or in the rough contests of strength and skill, women lived with a consuming loneliness that left a mark on them long after society and a settled world reached their door.

In their raw new homes of sod, log, adobe—small, crowded, often temporary dwellings—it was not a town house, a palace, a mansion they longed for but an extension and glorification of the agricultural pattern they knew—a bigger farmhouse with more rooms, fuller storehouses, finer stock, wider fields— and this they found in the plantation.

For pioneer women there was no joy or beauty in "scenic

grandeur." Rugged terrain, prairie wastes, towering mountains were only threats to their health and comfort and movement. They wanted a cozy terrain. With the exception of Mrs. Southworth, who rather liked a "wild gorge," most domestic novelists and their readers preferred the ideal they attempted, with some success, to reproduce in nature—a world with soft rolling hills, neat, well-fenced fields circled by tinkling brooks, and beyond the wooded glens and mossy dells smooth rivers gliding into placid lakes where pretty boats floated. The panther, the buffalo, the wolf and the bear gave way to a more decorative fauna, peacocks, swans, St. Bernards, browsing lambs, and Jersey cows. The lawn, the arbor, the geometrical bed, the twining vine possessed great importance.

Very early the domestic novelists evolved a system of spiritual botany wherein each plant had definite ethical properties. As early as *The Wide, Wide World* this esoteric knowledge of flowers was an important piece of feminine equipment. Little Ellen Montgomery was complimented on her decorations for a bier—". . . flowers of various kinds chosen, however, with exquisite taste and feeling. Beside the roses there were none that were not either white or distinguished for their fragrance . . . no yellow flowers, no purple, even the flaunting petunia though white had been left out by the nice hand that had culled them."

In *Rena; or, The Snowbird* Mrs. Hentz warned that a young lady who did not like flowers must be regarded with great suspicion. Such a confession implied almost total depravity.

The cultivated bloom, the rare exotic, became the sign and seal of the good woman's civilizing influence. She wore a few violets at her throat, some jasmin tucked in her belt; she dropped pansies and lillies as she went, on graves, in sickrooms, at balls, at meetings and partings. A single blossom crushed to the heart, pressed to the lips, embalmed in the pocketbook or merely enshrined in memory was enough to keep a good man on the right track or bring the most hardened sinner to repentance.

Elsie at Roselands and Viamede and Ion plucked camellias and fashioned bouquets and brought her dear papa, and less frequently her husband, the choicest bloom from her conservatory to adorn their buttonholes. Did she wish a lake, one was dug outside her drawing room and from her vine-covered portico delightful "prospects" met her eye on every side.

It was not the rose bowers, the sweeping carriage drives, the pillared verandas, the white cabins in the distance but the life they supported that enchanted readers. What woman did not envy Elsie? Mistress of a handsome establishment, well staffed by happy servants, with a fortune at her command, she dispensed hospitality, largesse, and advice with a generous hand to grateful recipients. The signs of wealth and luxury were everywhere—in satin damask hangings, inlaid boxes, handsomely bound books, rosewood pianofortes, striped silks and delicate muslins. Showers of gifts fell upon the deserving wellborn—ponies, gold watches, sets of pearls, lengths of real lace, silver spoons, complete wedding outfits—Elsie's generosity never slackened. The poor received soup and flannel and a Bible.

Life was a succession of picnics, visits, calls, parties and delightful excursions of every kind, with church on Sunday. For the short trips the family carriages were summoned, for longer journeys a yacht or a private car engaged. So little ever

177

disturbed the drowsy monotony of the narrative that after the first two books the series assumed the quality of a dream with all a dream's distortion. The time sequences went backward and forward; years were compressed into a paragraph and unimportant incidents spun out to a volume. Stories were told within stories within still other stories, characters were superimposed, the father and husband combined and divided, Elsie and her father were reproduced in later volumes in another parent and another child, Elsie's son-in-law, Captain Raymond and his daughter, Lulu, who re-enacted the old struggle; figures appeared and disappeared without explanation or reason; the plot through some kind of an inverted construction was resolved at the beginning of the series rather than the end. Elsie Dinsmore, herself, at eighty, surrounded by her children and grandchildren, remained a protected child who had never combed her own hair or put on her own slippers or raised her sweet voice. Yet she ruled her father, her husband, her children, and dominated her world with no other weapon than "love."

13 🌿 The Time of Victory

W<small>HILE</small> Elsie and her readers idled the hours away on the wide verandas of pillared mansions, out beyond the enchanted confines of Viamede and Roselands and Ion in the real world, strange things were happening.

An economic and social revolution set in motion by the Civil War raged furiously. The planter gave way to a new aristocrat, the businessman who had capital from his war profits, and friends in office and, through them, easy access to almost unlimited natural resources, for in 1860 nearly half the country was still "government land."

A fresh supply of laborers arrived in each vessel from abroad and these immigrants, added to the native born doubled the population every twenty-five years and created an assured domestic market for goods.

The shift from an agricultural to an industrial economy created a new rich and a new poor and, widening the economic and social difference between them, modified the old equalitarian tradition of pioneer life. The loneliness of the frontier gave way to a new kind of isolation—that of the dispossessed, footloose, unintegrated member of the new growing urban population.

The appearance of new manners and habits and ideas and equipment did not go unrecognized in popular fiction.

But the domestic novelists, like the majority of their contemporaries, understood little of the changes they recorded. The old agrarian ideal persisted. Real wealth and prestige came from land—a ducal estate, a rich plantation, or an anonymous but productive property somewhere in the background which provided its possessor with a handsome income. The professions, except for the ministry and occasionally the law, rated low in the social scale, the manufacture, except for an ironmaster, remained invisible; the merchant when he appeared was a retailer, often predestined to fail so that his wife might demonstrate her courage and acumen in improving the situation. Any fall of fortune invariably resulted from an absconding partner, intemperance, ill-health; while success came from prayer, early rising, a rich benefactor, a lucky accident—or some other factor equally divorced from economic law.

The older writers had little incentive to adapt their style or content to suit the changing times. The audience they won remained faithful. Augusta Evans received more than $100,000 in royalties in eight years. Mrs. Southworth stood first in popularity in 1872 among the patrons of the Boston Public Library. A survey at the end of that decade showed readers in Lawrence, Massachusetts, accorded her the same high place, with Caroline Lee Hentz and Mary Jane Holmes in close competition.

She was imitated, pirated and plagiarized. At least two other

Southworths traded on the magic name although they lacked as Mrs. Southworth called them, not only appropriated and "rewrote" her stories but even called upon her to supply them with a copy of the original "with as much nonchallence as . . . for a pattern for embroidery or a recipe for puddings." The Presbyterian Sunday School Board bought and published as new material and under a different name *Ishmael* to their embarrassment and Mrs. Southworth's rage.

The New York *Weekly*, the *Ledger's* main competitor, paid Mrs. Southworth's most successful imitator, May Agnes Fleming, $15,000 for two stories a year. Mrs. Fleming, a native of New Brunswick who lived in Brooklyn, like so many others had an intemperate husband and she supported herself and her children. She almost mechanized the production of the domestic novel. On May 1 each year she began a new story and wrote from exactly nine in the morning until noon each day for six weeks. To clear her mind between sessions she rode the stages up and down Broadway. The London *Journal* paid her well for the English rights to her work, and after serialization in the New York *Weekly* Carleton published her stories in book form and paid her 15 per cent royalty. She never approximated Mrs. Southworth's popularity but she left a fortune when she died at an early age in 1880.

Bonner increased Mrs. Southworth's stipend and continued his generous presents. Week by week through the years she sent in her weekly installments wherein brides continued to be deserted at the altar, children changed in their cradles, maniacs imprisoned in secret rooms, heiresses abducted and innocent youths falsely charged with crime. When she tired

181

of telling the story in a Southern setting she rang down another backdrop, a Scottish castle or perhaps a Duke's town house, but whatever the clime there was always a woman, rejected and betrayed—but eventually triumphant.

When, in Mrs. Southworth's second story, *Sybil Brotherton*, Sybil lost her estate, her old servant suggested, "Couldn't she teach the pianner or paint picters or diskiver some rich relations like the 'stressed ladies in the story books she used to read us about?" The latter usually proved the most practical solution.

Mrs. Holmes gave her heroines a little more of her own New England independence. Very frequently they supported themselves by teaching and articulated their grievances with spirit. The comparatively lower salaries women received, the sex and social prejudices of some boards, the meanness or indifference of examiners, the interference and distrust of parents evoked no sentimental repinings, but Mrs. Holmes, too, thought "diskivering" rich relatives preferable to working. In *Dora Deane; or, The East Indian Uncle* the latter comes to the rescue. Subsequent volumes provided a fashionable aunt, a brother back from the gold fields or—the very best solution for any economic problem—an affluent suitor and, the very best career for any woman, a good marriage.

Work after marriage was, of course, unthinkable—a horror reserved for the drunkard's wife. As St. Elmo told Edna Earl once she finally accepted him:

"To-day I snap the fetters of your literary bondage. There shall be no more books written! No more study, no more toil, no more anxiety, no more heartaches! And that dear public you love so well, must even help itself, and whistle for a new pet.

182

You belong solely to me now, and I shall take care of the life you have nearly destroyed, in your inordinate ambition. Come, the fresh air will revive you."

In 1868, Augusta Jane Evans married L. M. Wilson of Mobile, a widower older than her father, and like her heroines, Mrs. Wilson, too, abandoned her career.

"Because of her delicate health, Mr. Wilson objected to her writing," said a contemporary biographer, "and she discontinued it and devoted herself to the decoration of her homes and grounds." Or at least she did so until her eager publisher sent her a check for $25,000 as an advance, sight unseen, against any novel she would send him. Mr. Wilson was so pleased he displayed the check all over Mobile and his wife put on "the fetters of literary bondage" once again.

The same bait, althought offered in regrettably smaller amounts, lured other women, married and single, out of their homes to work for wages at a rapidly increasing rate. Among the newer writers who recognized and recorded this phenomenon was Miss Amanda Douglas of Mt. Pleasant, New Jersey.

Born in New York in 1831, Miss Douglas as a child met Thackeray and through relatives in Fordham became acquainted with Edgar Allan Poe, who made, she always said, an indelible impression upon her "with his large, dark eyes, modulated voice, he never laughed and seldom smiled."

His literary style did not influence her to the same degree. Miss Douglas' first success came in 1866 with *In Trust* which sold 20,000 copies. Thereafter she sat in a rocking chair "that fits me well" in her pretty study full of bric-a-brac, pictures, a profusion of magazines and pictures and turned out novels at the rate of one, sometimes two, a year for the next half century.

Her particular concern was the wellborn young woman suddenly impoverished who must find a way to support herself and some dependents and retain or regain a well-loved, rather pretentious home. Before she "diskivered the rich relations" or husband this young girl went out to work and seemingly employment was never too difficult to find—the real problem was how to reconcile the two disparate roles of wage earner and lady.

In *Home Nook,* published in 1873, Madge while waiting for her suitor to finish college considered working in a "fancy store" or learning dressmaking but decided her fiancé's aristocratic family might "remember it with a little sneer" later on. After discarding the possibility of earning a living from skeletonizing leaves and making pine-cone baskets, she turned to teaching which she disliked but:

> It was not only herself she must think of, but Mrs. Westlake's daughter-in-law. To be lowered in the social scale would be worse than the burden of poverty.

True, she did not teach very long. Two unexpected fortunes and a rich husband improved the family's situation. Madge meantime designed a pretty stained-glass window "the brilliant colors most artistically arranged and the design perfect." On the strength of this and a notebook full of drawings "of odd rooms, nooks and corners" she gave up teaching and became an architect.

Picturesque or dramatic ways for heroines to earn money were preferred then as now. In *A Woman's Inheritance* in

1885 Christmas Ormiston, who inherited a nearly bankrupt factory, saved the business by discovering in a secret drawer a new and cheap way to make fine paper.

Although admittedly far from usual this girl had been trained to work. As she explained to her new friend:

"I do not expect to do much with society. Papa began to educate me for the business after he was hurt, and it was his desire I should carry it on."

"But you could not. A lady cannot manage rough, insolent workmen. And it is not refined or womanly. Would you not be afraid?"

Despite frequent warnings that women in business would "lose their high faith, their delicacy, nay even that fine purity that is as the bloom of the unplucked grape," Christmas Ormiston went to the mill each day; she helped in the laboratory and the office, she learned to keep the accounts, even to bargain with disgruntled workmen. In the concluding pages it was the idle society girl who lost her bloom and "pure souled, high minded, nobly formed" Christmas who won the hero.

Perhaps Amanda Douglas in her twenty-fourth book, *Out of the Wreck*, sounded the knell of the domestic novel. The elements of that tale had appeared a hundred times before. Thomas Marshall lost his business and taking to drink mistreated his three children, consorted with barmaids, and squandered his wife's pittance. She did little praying or pleading and even less weeping. When it became obvious her husband would not reform, Mrs. Marshall left him and started a millinery business. It was not easy. Her friends and relatives believed, as did her mother-in-law:

that it was a woman's highest mission to suffer in silence. Only a coarse, ignoble soul could make an outcry. Had this come to her she would have allowed herself to be tortured into the grave before she would have made a move towards extricating herself. What God sent upon her must be borne meekly, uncomplainingly. Her beautiful resignation would have filled her friends with admiration and her memory would have been kept green by tales of her devotion.

Mrs. Marshall disagreed:

". . . It may be heresy, but I begin to think one law binding upon both. I cannot understand why I must live a miserable, distasteful life of privation to be shut out of all the society for which my early training fitted me, to be shunned like a moral leper when the crime is his. I think I have a right . . . to rescue myself and my children. I will not plunge farther down that black fearful gulf."

Her shop prospered. She made friends and saw her children well established in life. When her husband came home rich and repentant she nursed him through his last illness but neither his money nor his belated reformation made much difference to her.

Out of the Wreck bore the subtitle *Or Was It a Victory?* Author and reader answered in the affirmative.

Changing times not only made new poor but new rich and the problem of the latter was how to reconcile Christian ethics with mounting profits. Isabella MacDonald Alden, better known as Pansy, considered this problem throughout what was probably one of the longest careers in American letters. In 1851, at the age of ten, her father had a short story

186

of hers printed in the local paper. In her early girlhood she won first prize in a Sunday-school story contest for her novel, *Helen Lester*, and as she often said, "thereafter I was never idle." She prepared the primary lessons for the *Westminister Teacher*; she edited the Presbyterian *Primary Quarterly*; she published a children's magazine entitled *Pansy*; she wrote a serial story every winter for the *Herald and Presbyter*; she taught a Sunday-school class of one hundred children; she married a minister and assisted him in parish work; she raised a family; and, as she once said, "whenever anything went wrong I just went upstairs and wrote a book about it," over one hundred and twenty-five in all, the last, *An Interrupted Night*, with an introduction by her niece, Grace Livingston Hill, published in 1929, the year before her death.

Hers were the domestic novels of piety in the tradition of Susan Warner, Marion Harland and Martha Finley but women now concerned themselves with social as well as spiritual matters and extended their sphere of influence from the home to the community.

Increasing industrialization and the rapid growth of cities was giving every town in the United States a slum. No one could help but see poverty, and the crime, filth, disease, cruelty and ignorance it bred. Those with a conscience tried to solve the problem of how to acquire and keep great wealth, a basic of American life, and at the same time practice the principles of Christianity.

The old pot of soup, glass of jelly benevolence could no longer suffice. A broader program of social service was required. The heroines of *Pansy* tried the winning ways that

187

had proved so effective with husbands and fathers upon the slum urchins and young workingmen in various industries. In the pages of the novels they seemed as effective.

. . . Mrs. Roberts aimed at nothing less formidable than the teaching of these boys to read and write; and knew as well as you or I know it, that to frankly own that she was ready and willing to give her time and patience to so teaching them would be to outwit herself. They did not belong to the class who can be beguiled into evening schools. . . . these were lower in the scale. . . . it required diplomacy; and no people can be more diplomatic, on occasion, than certain most innocent-looking little women. Mrs. Roberts had studied her way step by step. . . . she led the way to a discussion of different styles of writing, bringing forth to aid her a certain old autograph album which had been to many places of note, among others Chautauqua, and had the names of distinguished persons. . . .

Several pages later the young reprobates have been coaxed into experimenting with pen and ink and the worst of the lot won over with "Colson here has made the only respectable R-curve there is in the company."

This flattering discovery brings a "glow" on the boy's face, "a momentary transformation" which calls up from Mrs. Roberts the inspiration for the meeting, "a soft whisper heard by one ear alone:—Thank God."

Before long, writing lessons interspersed with poetry reading, elocution lessons, some experimentation with that novelty the typewriter win the young men to paths of respectability.

But in other instances the charitable impulse seemed less well applied. A poor young girl was made happy and satisfied in her lot by being treated to an edifying lecture on temperance, brought home to enjoy a night in the hostess' elegant pink room, described in glowing terms by the author:

The walls were tinted with what might be called a suggestion of pink, with just a touch of sunset gold about the mouldings.

The carpet was soft and rich; it gave back no sound of footfall. It was strewn with pink buds; some just opening into beauty, some half-blown. Accustomed to the sight of elegant carpets as you are, you would almost have stooped to pick one of these buds, they looked so real. The curtains to the windows were white, but lined with rose pink . . . looped back with knots of pink and white drapery; so was the dressing-bureau. The easy-chairs were upholstered in soft grays with a pinkish tinge; and the tidies, lavishly displayed, were all of pink and white.

Although the girl privileged to enjoy the delights of the pink room confesses "I never knew much about Heaven. . . . I had a kind of notion . . . it was rich folks and grand folks like you" when her hostess kindly explains that she has been invited to enjoy Heaven as she has the pink room and continues "with tender words and simple illustrations the 'old, old story' so fitted to the wants of the world," the result could usually be predicted:

It was midnight when they knelt together, the fair child of luxury and the child of poverty; but the Saviour, who intercedes for both, bent His ear, and heard again the cry of a groping soul, seeking Him out of darkness, and held out His loving, never-failing arms, able to reach down to her depth, and received her to himself. Who can tell that story? Who can describe how Heaven seemed to the girl just then?

No one perhaps—but to the heroine and her author it was

obviously another and larger "pink" room whose inhabitants they were privileged to select.

If by chance the attempts to rescue the impoverished slum dwellers from their environment and their fate came too late:

If . . . the wretched bed, with its distressing rags, were turned out together, and a comfortable one took its place. Broths and teas and jellies and physical comfort of every kind were furnished, and the doctor did his best to battle with the disease that long years of want and misery had fastened upon their victim. It was all to late, of course. It was true, what Mr. Roberts sadly said, that half of the effort, expended years or even months before, might have saved the poor, tortured life; but now!

There was usually time enough left to effect a quick conversion for such an unfortunate being, who then died, and the next day

there was a hearse, and a minister. . . . Dirk and his sister, in neat apparel, came out together and were seated in Mr. Roberts' carriage; and all the boys of the Monday-evening Class walked arm in arm after the slow-moving carriages; and the children of the alley stopped their playing and their fighting, and the women stood silent in doorways, and took, most of them, their very first lesson in the proprieties of life.

"She's got a ride in a carriage at last, poor soul!" said one, thinking of the worn-out-body in the coffin. . . . But the scene made its impression, and left its lesson.

Although just what the lesson was the novelists may not have fully understood.

And as late as 1885 Pansy was still attempting to resolve this problem for herself and her readers. Her novel *One*

Commonplace Day is the story of a woman who decides to live her life according to the text "Whether, therefore, ye eat or drink or whatsoever ye do, do all to the glory of God." She went

down the long, wide, old-fashioned, hall, and threw open the door of her quaintly-finished dining-room. The table was neatly laid for one, and glistened with china and shone with silver, and was beautiful with choice, fine drapery; Miss Hannah's breakfast table was always a picture pleasant to look at. Through the half-open door came a whiff of fragrant coffee, and a hint of broiling steak . . .

"There it is!" said Miss Hannah, "whether ye eat or drink. How, I should like to know! To be sure, it will strengthen me for my day's work, I suppose, to eat my steak and drink my coffee; and I am thankful to God for the food to eat, and the pleasant place to eat it in; but how can I plan the day's work so as to match the directions?"

It occurred to her that her long-time and faithful gardener looked hungry and, when inquiry proved this correct, she ordered another servant to "cut a large piece of the steak, and pour a cup of coffee, and arrange things on the table by the window, and have Peter come in at once and eat a good breakfast, and fill the willow basket with whatever there is that will do for it—that cold chicken, and the bowl of broth, pour that into a tin pail, and put in bread, and a glass of grape jelly, and have Peter take it over to his house as soon as he has eaten his breakfast."

—a reasonable price to pay, it would seem, for the luxuries Miss Hannah could then enjoy. Throughout the book Miss Hannah debated whether she should use lace curtains, ruffles on her dress, "her handsome old-fashioned family carriage drawn by two shining horses and Peter who had been installed as coachman . . . in a new suit." The last named was justified in a chapter entitled "The Proof of the Divine Hand" when she found herself:

in the Flats which seem to have sprung up with the coming of the railroad . . . a part of the town almost utterly unknown . . . yet human beings lived there and were huddled together in disgraceful crowds. . . . Down one of the filthy narrow alleys went the high-stepping sleek horses and handsome carriage. Some of the children threw mud and some of them threw up their arms in a vain effort to frighten the horses and all of them stared. . . . Suddenly she gave a low startled explanation and a quick order, "Peter, stop here."

She had seen a shabbily dressed man . . . coming out of the door. It was this man and the burden he carried which had called forth . . . the startled order for he had under his arm a small pine box, unpainted, unadorned in any way, yet unmistakably serving as a last resting place for some one's dead. There followed him the most haggard-faced woman Miss Wainwright's eyes had ever seen. There were no tears on the face; she looked like one who had shed all her tears years before, and who had now nothing but settled despair with which to meet any calamity.

"Here," said Miss Wainwright, leaning from her carriage and speaking in the tone of quiet command which generally produces obedience, "bring it here!" and she tossed the cusions right and left, making room for the small coffin.

A minister she summoned for the occasion (proving again the necessity of her carriage) summed up the situation: "A little coffin," he said, in low, sympathetic tones. "Another baby rescued from the sin, and the sorrow, and the danger of this dangerous world." The child's father, remembering what can only be described as happier funerals, where there had been a white casket, and silver adornments, and nodding plumes, and costly flowers, and dirge-like music, and many carriages . . . the funeral of his little brother . . . he remembered his mother's tears, and knew that she had shed bitterer ones for him even before she died than any which fell on that coffin.

"Better in there," he said, nodding his head toward the pine box, and speaking in a husky voice, "Better in there than to live to be such a man as I."

And the mother . . . suddenly buried her head in the folds of her ragged shawl and sobbed as though her poor heart would break. They were the first tears she had shed. . . . She lived so far away from the sound of Heaven that not a thought of its beauty, its rest and the little children gathered there had come to her since her own childhood when she knew it well.

Children dying or dead had long played an important part in the domestic novel; the former extracted temperance pledges, made converts, reconciled parents and resolved many plots, while the latter continued their influence from the grave—comforting the good, haunting the guilty, softening the brutal.

So frequently did the clichés of grief appear—the lock of hair, the shoe, the sun's last rays on the fading cheek, the plaintive voice asking, "Will Papa come home?"—that some later readers found amusement in these bits of sentimentality, while others unfamiliar with the vital statistics of the nineteenth century concluded that this preoccupation with dead and dying children symbolized a rejection of maternity. Certainly, families of ten, twelve and fourteen, not uncommon in real life, became the exception in the American domestic novel. Two or three children seemed to the writers, and apparently to their readers, a better number. It was not that women refused maternity. The childless were objects of pity, of veiled contempt, almost in a class with eccentric old maids, but women had perhaps realized that if a choice were possible a small family in the home was preferable to a larger one in the graveyard.

There was a reason why readers demanded—and writers repeated—again and again these harrowing accounts of dying children. Of all the grievances nineteenth-century feminists had or thought they had, a real and terrible one lurked in the old, worn phrases: "raised seven and lost seven," "thirteen children . . . four here and nine in heaven," "I kept two of my eight." If a woman was to endure this double tragedy— the loss of a precious individual and the negation of her creativity not once but repeatedly—and remain sane, the experience must be given some form and meaning—softened, lightened, hallowed, transmuted—to the degree that words and phrases and conceptions can perform such alchemy.

The domestic novel offered this glorification in the child only lent by God, the baby angel, the fading flower, the little ones too good for the world's wickedness, the Frankies and Effies and Charlies and Nellies remembered by the tiny rosebud, the golden curl, the crumbled shoe, the dented locket— gone to met again in a happier place. These were the key words to loose easy tears and unrepressed grief, the ideas to dim the reality of children's dying before they had a chance to live and dead with such cruel dying—burnt by fever, wrung by dystentery and diarrhea, strangled by diphtheria and croup, agonizing their small lives away while mothers stood by helpless to keep them or ease the pain of their going.

The Time of Victory

In an antiseptic and sterile world where prenatal care, trained obstetricians, preventive medicine, prepared formulas, public health measures have reduced infant mortality to less than 5 per cent these are legendary horrors, almost forgotten. We can afford restraint and rationalization and speak of "constructive grief." Another age will show us where *our* sentimentality exists. For it is always a cloak to hide the face of horror, and wherever we perceive sentimentality we may know that beneath it lies some unbearable truth we did not dare meet face to face.

The introduction of a dead child as a justification for keeping a carriage apparently did not seem illogical or in questionable taste to Pansy's readers. Sincerely and eagerly, if sometimes ineptly, they tried to do good in the only way they knew.

Later in the same volume Pansy's heroine turned her efforts to the cause of temperance. In this work she was joined by an incipient social service worker, who described her own methods to Miss Hannah:

"If I had money, I should have rented the room and fitted it up nice and homelike and hired a nice homelike old man to come and keep it, and had it a bright, clean lounging place for the boys who were not so far astray but that they could appreciate its clean, bright looks and ways. But I hadn't the money, you see, so I had to do the best I could.

"Oh! you needn't look shocked; I am no would-be reformer trying to turn the world upside down; mixing white with black, until a looker-on can't tell which is which. I remember that I'm a woman. I can't invite them in, poor fellows, and give them a pitying word now and then as I'd like to. I have to keep my doors closed and locked. But all day and all the evening I keep my shades up. There's a room up-stairs where I sit and sew; but downstairs there isn't a soul to be seen; only a cheery fire in the grate, and a round table with a red cloth on, in the middle of the room, and a newspaper on it, and the big old Bible that my father used to read out of, and a rocking-chair at the left and a little smaller chair just the other side, both of them empty; and the room as bright as a good-sized lamp will make it. It's a picture, don't you see? I don't know how many poor fellows who stagger by, had homes like it once, where maybe the mothers and fathers sat and waited for them; sometimes I think it is a good thing that the chairs always have to be empty, because they will remind some of them all the plainer that the mothers and fathers are gone.

"Well, there I keep the room, looking as much like a picture of a neat plain home as I can, and I stretch the shades just as high as I can, and then I go up-stairs and make buttonholes, and pray that the Lord will use the one clean place on this street, somehow, for his glory. I have to leave the 'How' with him. But the chairs won't always be empty, I hope and pray. I want to get acquainted with wives and mothers, and get them to trusting me, and then when they come hunting their treasures who are lost in this street, I want them to learn to slip in here and wait and watch, and if they can get hold of the husband or the son, to drop into this clean spot with him, and try to coax him back. I don't know what will come of it, I am sure. It is the best thing I could plan, and I am trying it. I have only been here a month. . . . I want to have a little something to tempt them with; an apple, or a bite of cake if I can manage it, or even a bit of candy now and then."

The same year Pansy published *One Commonplace Day* a group of trade unionists in Chicago began agitating for higher wages and an eight-hour day. Not even the Haymarket

Riots that spring nor the suppression of the Homestead Strike six years later could stop the growth of the organized labor movement. Life had grown too complex for amateur reformers.

The apple, the bite of cake, the bit of candy would no longer suffice for men—nor for women. A new way of life had begun.

14 ❦ Common Sense
in the Household

IN OCTOBER, 1886, the final chapters of Mrs. Southworth's *A Deed Without a Name* appeared in the *Ledger*. She had written forty-six novels in the thirty-eight years. Bonner, grown older and stouter and after the tragic death of his wife and daughter less daring and ambitious, inquired if his old friend and contributor felt "played out."

Her answer was quick and vehement:

What in the—*Dexter* do you mean by—'played out' in the remotest connection with me?

I tell ye what Brither Bab!—when all the rest of me is played out, my heart and brain and hand will do their work and do it well while ever they have work to do—Please the Lord.

Despite her protests, Mrs. Southworth for the first time did not have a new book in progress. In 1887 the *Ledger* re-ran *Only a Girl's Heart* which had first appeared in its pages twelve years earlier. But although Mrs. Southworth condensed and revised the tale to suit the changing style, the reports as it progressed were not enthusiastic.

Mrs. Southworth wrote Bonner:

I was surprised that your reader did not think sixteen as good as fifteen. I thought it better. There was no more dialogue in it than necessary to develop plot and character. I wrote that number twice over—gave every day and evening of six days to it. Close attention to details is a quality I share with the best authors. . . . But I go into no more detail than is expedient. I have always tried to please the multitude and satisfy the cultured and with what success others may judge. I know that I number among my readers some professors of colleges, ministers of the gospel and senators on the one hand—School boys and girls and little street gamins on the other and a vast multitude between. I always do my very best; but it is utterly impossible for me to write in any other way than my own. As I do like criticism, I must accept the adverse as willingly as the favorable—if I can. . . . Faithfully yours, E.D.E.N. Southworth. P.S. If I could change my nature and write differently I would do it—for your sake, if you wished it. E.D.E.N.S.

That same year Bonner accepted a serial from a young woman new to the *Ledger's* pages. Her name was Laura Jean Libbey, she lived in Brooklyn and her career had begun five years earlier when at seventeen, accompanied by a friend, she walked across the Bridge to New York and sold a short story for $25 to one of Bonner's many competitors, George Munro, editor of the *Fireside Companion*. With a portion of this sudden wealth the new author bought five pounds of marshmallows which she and her friend consumed until overcome by nausea on the return trip home.

When Laura Jean Libbey came to the *Ledger* she promised, "I will write young love stories—pure, bright—with a vein of deep romance and pathos running through them—a story for the masses." But her work did not quite please Bonner. She was late with her copy, an unpardonable sin, on the pretext "I always believe in taking *time* for laying out a good

199

plot, it pays in the end." She was repetitious—and when Bonner pointed out that two of her stories had similar plots, she denied the charge with rather more pert self-assurance than Bonner's contributors customarily showed.

Bonner did not care. The enthusiasm he once expended on the *Ledger* now went into his stable of fast horses. In 1887 he resigned and left his sons in charge of the paper.

Mrs. Southworth's long career was over, too. The *Ledger* ran *The Malediction*, one of her earlier books, again and reprinted for a third and last time *Only a Girl's Heart*.

A woman alone in the nineteenth century, no matter how attractive the role seemed to the domestic novelists, had a difficult time. Mrs. Southworth supported, in addition to her own son and daughter, her mother, her sister Lotty, "the parlor favorite" in their childhood, her half sister and brother-in-law, the Badens, and their large family of children.

The *Ledger* contract certainly gave Mrs. Southworth more economic security than the majority of workingwomen enjoyed but at the sacrifice of great physical and creative energy. The mere mechanics of preparing the manuscript took hours. Week after week she went back and forth to the post office mailing copy, picking up proofs, answering the readers' questions, writing Bonner, checking copy, wrapping and mailing the bulky parcels. (Mrs. Southworth always claimed she invented the manila clasp envelope to simplify this task.) Each installment was hand-copied at least twice and if, as frequently happened, it were lost en route, the whole thing had to be done over, sometimes from memory, and rushed to New York. This anxiety plagued Mrs. Southworth's life.

200

"Let me know if the manuscript was safely received," she implored the editors in almost every letter.

The speed at which she wrote precluded any attempt to develop style. The amount she finally produced exhausted even her fertile imagination. The necessity, too, for each chapter to end on a note of suspense made any real plot or unity of construction impossible. Her readers preferred action to the development of character. To desert the *Ledger*, which meant Bonner, was unthinkable.

The promise Mrs. Southworth showed in *Retribution* she never fulfilled. It may be that, like many writers, she had one, and only one, story to tell, or perhaps if she had been less a woman, less bound by devotion to her family and gratitude to her rescuer, she might have been more an artist.

Mrs. Southworth once said she had never met a person who did not know her work. Fifty years after her death in 1899 her books, many still in print, commanded an audience.

Schools were making more and more readers but the story papers found them hard to please. As people acquired education and experience they demanded subtlety, sophistication, artistry and style. Now almost the only newly literate were the unskilled and untaught—immigrants, freedmen, a few others perhaps from very isolated areas without public schools. Critics had always sneered that the domestic novels as well as the story papers were read by servant girls. Until well after the Civil War there were not enough servants in the United States to buy an appreciable number of books— even if they had wished to spend half their weekly wage on a single volume.

By the end of the eighties this familiar charge had acquired some basis in fact. The swell of immigration brought "servant girls" and other unskilled laborers in droves and, although their wages remained pitifully small, they could afford the paperbacked editions of the more popular novels which sold for a dime, sometimes a nickel.

Laura Jean Libbey did not stay long at the *Ledger*. Its circulation, like that of all the story papers, was falling and Miss Libbey, as she told Bonner, wanted to write "for the masses" and this she proceeded to do. She had all the necessary qualifications. She was a fast and tireless worker. Dr. Louis Gold, who in his youth served for a short time as Miss Libbey's amanuensis, reported that she began dictating at nine o'clock in the morning and without an outline she composed fluently with few breaks until noon, stopping only to throw open the door from time to time to see if she might catch a servant listening. At this rate she could produce sixty to ninety pages of foolscap manuscript sheets a week.

She was a realist, a practical woman of affairs who knew the difference between fiction and real life. Albert Payson Terhune, Marion Harland's son, while a reporter on the New York *Evening World* went to interview Miss Libbey shortly after her marriage to Van Mater Stilwell, a lawyer. Workmen were busy redecorating the house and during Terhune's visit one cut his hand severely.

"Give the poor fellow a swallow of whisky," said Miss Libbey, with great presence of mind, "and send quick for the doctor."

Terhune reminded his hostess that in one of her novels

when a similar accident occurred the heroine offered her own alabaster arm for a blood transfusion.

"That's all right enough in novels," Miss Libbey explained, "but in real life whisky is good enough—for plumbers."

For all their flights of fancy, their miraculous coincidences, their contrived plots, Mrs. Southworth, Mrs. Holmes, Mrs. Hentz and their colleagues brought some sincerity to their work. They took themselves seriously. They respected their readers. Miss Libbey did not. She made no attempt to create character. Every one of her books followed the same stylized form.

The heroine, a young girl between sixteen and nineteen, with fair curls, fair skin, blue eyes often tear-swollen, little white hands and a dainty, spritelike form, hurried through page one on her way to find or perform work that would enable her to support a beloved dependent.

On page two a bold, dark-eyed villain feasted his gaze on this innocent beauty and with a twirl of his mustache accosted her with an improper proposal. At the top of page three he was overheard by a tall, handsome, fair-faced young man who reprimanded such insolence with a well-directed blow from a strong muscular arm. By pages five and six the two other stock characters had made their appearance, a poor girl who loves the villain and an heiress intent on marrying the hero. For the next two hundred pages the heroine, who usually bore a diminutive—Little Lottie, Little Faynie, Little Leafy—was shunted between the other four characters with all the speed, precision and passion of an empty freight car. She was chloroformed, gassed and smothered, sprayed with acid and poison, blown up by gunpowder, borne down by the churning wheels of a ferry. She was tied to a railroad track, thrown from a cliff, imprisoned in a madhouse and kidnaped. She was stabbed, choked, buried, dug up and carried to the dissecting room and, at the very moment the scalpel descended, revived by a bolt of lightning. From all these trials Little Gay or Dorothy or Rose emerged unscathed and able to murmur, "The course of true love never did run smooth."

That Miss Libbey knew exactly whom she was writing for is easily discerned from her titles *Only a Mechanic's Daughter, Willful Gaynell; or, The Little Beauty of the Passaic Cotton Mills, Lotta, the Beautiful Cloak Model, or Pretty Madcap Dorothy; or, How She Won a Lover, A Romance of the Jolliest Girl in the Book Bindery* and *A Magnificent Love Story of the Life of a Beautiful, Wilful New York Working Girl.*

Although these working girls all found fortunes, they remembered their origin. After Willful Gaynell's adoption by a rich man she said:

"I am only a working girl . . . I shall never feel above them; my heart will always be with them.

"God bless you, my child," returned the old millionaire banker warmly, "your heart is in the right place. I honor you for those brave words. My wife was a working girl . . . she always tells me she don't feel one whit more of a lady in her silks and satins than she did in her neat print dress and spotless apron."

Miss Libbey continued:

When the mill girls heard the news they all exclaimed; "Oh, it seems just like a beautiful novel . . ."

204

And a rousing cheer went up from the honest hearts of the mill hands, for the girl who had been one amongst them, who had suffered all their hardships, knew their privations and what it was to eat the bread of toil, receiving her wages so gratefully in the little envelope when Saturday night came.

Little Gay would be a great lady now, they well knew; but they knew, too, she could never be proud and cold, would be in the future what she had been in the past, the stanch, true friend of the noble working girls.

Laura Jean Libbey's novels seldom, if ever, received a serious review, but she had a gift for acquiring public notice. She called on booksellers, she wrote a column of advice for a newspaper, she appeared on the vaudeville stage, she traveled around the country and graciously gave interviews whenever she could find a reporter as impressionable as the one in Missouri who wrote:

Miss Libbey and her mother were assigned to one of the most comfortable rooms in the hotel, and after dinner they made a hasty visit to the chief points of interests in St. Joseph, including, of course, the book-stores, where the fair authoress's works are meeting with ready sale.

A representative of "The Herald" last evening sent his card up to Miss Libbey by "Front", and she cheerfully accorded him an interview. The reporter was ushered into the parlor, and in a few minutes the charming young authoress entered. Her presence in the room was like that of a rainbow after a storm. There was a cordial welcome, a fraternizing, as if both had been acquainted for years. Miss Laura Jean gracefully wheeled a chair in position for the reporter, and then gracefully seated herself upon an ottoman in front of him.

Her eyes are a fortune to her, for they are the most expressive that ever gazed upon an interviewer; they gleam and sparkle while she talks, indicating the change of thought or fancy which takes place in her mind while conversing, before she has time to express it in words. "I am ever so glad you have called upon me," she said, and before a question could be asked she continued, "Mother and I are taking a little pleasure trip. That is to be construed in this way: Mother's health is bad and we decided to go to the mountains—to Denver—and see if she could not get some relief."

"Have you visited any one in St. Joseph today?" was asked.

"No one except the booksellers. Our stay here has necessarily been very short. Yet I've fallen in love with your city, and on our return from Denver, we will stop and have a long visit and get acquainted. St. Joseph is one of the most progressive cities in the West. Notwithstanding this has been a rainy, gloomy day, I've been taking notes. I have noticed your preparations to illuminate the hill-tops with lights from the electric towers, as the Indians of yore did with brush-piles. Your signals, however, will be of a different nature—signals showing the advancement of science and the enterprise of St. Joseph."

Miss Libbey is an authoress of no mean rank, and has sprung into prominence as a writer which classes her with the best of modern novelists. On the preface of the "Pretty Young Girl," she says: "I write of men as I find them—loyal, noble, brave, with a chivalrous reverence for true womanhood, and who hold that purity in women is the rosebloom that jewels her existence."

"One of the highest compliments ever paid me," said Miss Libbey to the reporter, as he was leaving the parlor, "was by 'The American,' of Nashville, when it said, 'The male sex owes a gift of gratitude to Miss Libbey.' "

Miss Libbey wrote plays, short sketches and edited a semivanity publication and charged contributors well for the honor of appearing in it. When Albert Payson Terhune, on behalf of his editor, asked her to do a column for the *Evening*

World she told him her rates were 25 cents a word. Terhune, shocked, reminded her that Rudyard Kipling and Anthony Hope did not receive this.

"Anthony Hope and Rudyard Kipling," Miss Libbey repeated in high disdain. "When did either of them write a book that sold like my *Ione, the Pride of the Mill,* or *Leonie Locke*? When did either of them earn sixty thousand dollars a year? That's *my* income."

Mrs. Holmes's place on the New York *Weekly* was occupied by Bertha M. Clay, who was not even a living personality. There had once been an Englishwoman, Charlotte Mary Braeme or Brame, who wrote under this name but after her death a succession of men turned out these novels for Street and Smith.

New novels by Mrs. Holmes still delighted readers. She continued to published until shortly before her death in 1907. The life and times and manners she chronicled with considerable accuracy and artistry had vanished.

Whether or not the domestic novelists knew it, the world had changed. The demands of the women at Seneca Falls were being granted—some, it is true, more slowly than others. The right to vote was still a generation away, but each year more women went out of their homes to work. In every state they had a tacit if not a full legal right to control their property and person and usually in a divorce or separation they received custody of their children. They excercised an increasing control over the churches, the schools, the cultural life of the country. They spent more and more of the family income.

Marion Harland, at the beginning of her career, conscious

of a mission, thought, as she said in the dedication in *Alone,* that she could "best promote the happiness and usefulness of my kind" by writing novels. Twenty-five years later she was not so sure this was the best way to achieve her goal.

"I don't think," she said in interviews, "my novels did any harm," although she added that if she had it to do over she would "boil my novels down and write fewer. I wrote my first book at seventeen—a thing I should certainly never allow a daughter of mine to do."

In *True as Steel* in 1872 she drew a devastating portrait of the heroine's mother, a confirmed addict of the sentimental novel.

With one foot she rocked the cradle . . . Her right hand held a purple-covered novel, dog-eared and dirty from the many fingers through which it had passed. In the left was a half-lemon, which she dipped from time to time in a cup of sugar on the candle-stand beside her. And while she sucked at the tart confection, she read at her book, and rocked at her baby . . . on whose sticky face divers flies . . . were rioting.

When this diet produced "mental dyspepsia by overheating the imagination," Mrs. Todd "kept her bed and lived upon candy, Eugene Sue and Laudanum."

In this same novel Marion Harland ridiculed the dedicated pious heroines, such as Fleda in *Queechy,* who spent "three-fourths of her time in getting up omellettes, hashed chicken and potato-puffs for the delectation of . . . Carleton." "Cold chicken, bread and butter, cake and wine set out in five minutes," Mrs. Terhune thought, "is more inspiriting and to the point than a duodecimo volume of sympathetic blank verse or a butt full of such sweet rain as is given out by the melting eyes—the aqueducts of brimming hearts."

In 1871, Marion Harland wrote a new kind of book, *Common Sense in the Household*. Other cookbooks, needless to say, existed. Eliza Leslie and Catharine Beecher had both written popular ones, but as Mrs. Terhune pointed out, the former "lived all her life in a boarding house" and the latter had neither husband nor children.

Mrs. Terhune wrote her guide from practical experience. "I didn't know anything when I got married," she said, "how to dust or make a bed. I washed the first steak. My husband often said he had five servants and one slave, his wife." She soon learned how to manage a household, care of her children, she bore six, help her husband in the duties of his large parish and pursue her own career. Hers was the first book to treat homemaking as a skilled and dignified profession.

Carleton, who published her novels, refused the book—it was so revolutionary in concept—and only after considerable persuasion did Mr. Scribner, a friend of the Terhunes, agree to bring it out.

Sales were enormous and Marion Harland's royalties, her old friend and former publisher, J. C. Derby, said, "were three times as much as the Governor of New York's salary." The domestic novel had served its purpose and the time had come for common sense in the household.

Epilogue

All the Happy Endings

The women who wrote the domestic novel are gone—a footnote in a textbook, a chapter in a dissertation mark their literary resting place. Only Mrs. Stowe commands any continued interest. While one critic contends her important books were trivia another discovers her trivia had importance.

Mrs. Stowe and her contemporaries brought varying degrees of talent and intelligence to their task but one thing they all shared—a dissatisfaction and a drive. They worked, and worked hard, to make a place for themselves in a man's world.

The domestic novels gather dust in attics and thrift shops. The handsome gilt duodecimo bindings have faded and the paper backs, grown brown and brittle, dissolve in a curious hand. Yet a surprising number of people, principally women, still read and enjoy these relics of another world. Few titles remained in print after the paper shortage grew acute during the last war, but antiquarian book dealers have a steady, if not brisk trade, in some of the old favorites.

The intricate plots, the high-flown dialogue, the violent action made no lasting impressions. A character or two, an incident remain in the conscious folk memory—Little Eva with Uncle Tom, Little Elsie fainting at the piano, Little

Ellen selecting the fittings for her writing desk—but who remembers Charlotte Temple, Edna Earl, Tempest and her sister Sunshine, or Ida Lacy? American women eventually made themselves into the glorious creatures of their own imagination and convinced the world that beauty, youth and spirit were national characteristics—but Capitola the archetype is quite forgotten.

Nonetheless many women who never sighed or cried over a domestic novel still live as if they were the heroine of one. Emotional responses, patterns of sex relationships, the "proper" role of male and female are handed down in families like other heirlooms. Few indeed are the living women so "advanced," so "rational" they have not on some occasion played the Angelic Martyr, the Divine Goddess, the Indispensable Woman, or the Long-suffering Wife.

The twentieth century has its own brand of domestic fiction. The form has changed. The "home service" magazine replaces the story papers; radio serials, television plays, motion pictures encroach on the "circulating library novel," but the content remains much the same.

It still takes more courage than many women can muster to love a whole man. So the emasculation process continues, and blindness, amnesia, paralysis are now chronic afflictions for heroes. Father is reduced from the dignity of a monster to the role of a hapless, helpless clown, a court jester to his wife and children.

Women achieved their independence—almost absolute control over their person, their property, their children; the right to live and work, to marry and have families, or not, as they pleased. Was that the happy ending? Unfortunately, very seldom and for very few, not even for the women who yearned and struggled the hardest for their "rights."

Freedom is a strange, wild, frightening thing—hard to understand, to accept, to use, to share, to keep. In the degree and manner that women suffered they repaid the score, and took *their* turn at being selfish, domineering, inconstant, intemperate, ruthless, and often surpassed their instructors.

Perhaps they may be excused. The provocation was great— as the violence of the retaliation proves. Years of repression and frustration cannot be forgotten within one or even two generations.

Has the time come for a masculine counterattack or should the victors press their advantage and exact higher and higher tribute? Who rules best? Apart from their functions in procreation what is the role of a man and a woman in society and in marriage? Now we need not find one answer for all women and another for all men.

For slowly and inefficiently the old social patterns do dissolve and resolve into new ones and a different and better kind of sex relationship begins to appear—the possibility of a true partnership that makes the fullest use of each individual and his particular gifts to complement and sustain and fulfill and advance the entity. Then, when at last whole men and whole women are free to love as equals, they will find the real happy ending.

BIBLIOGRAPHICAL ADDENDA

My primary source of information was the domestic novels themselves. Their authors were many and prolific and since it would be impossible within a single volume to consider, even to list by name, all their works, I had, of necessity, to be somewhat arbitrary in my choice.

I omitted writers who had only one or two popular books to their credit, such for example as Miriam Coles Harris, who never repeated the success she made with her *Rutledge*. A few juveniles—Sophie May's *Dottie Dimples* was one—who became best sellers but I discarded books written for, although not always those eventually read by, the very young. Writers who reached their largest audience in periodicals—Mrs. Harriet Lewis of the *Ledger* might be sighted as an instance—were also left out. Finally and with great reluctance I eliminated the English domestic novelists although Charlotte Mary Yonge, Mrs. Henry Wood, Mary E. Braddon, The Duchess and many others sold extremely well in the United States.

Exclusion proved far easier than inclusion. I wanted to consider the most popular American domestic novels but popularity, relative or exact, is impossible in some cases, difficult in all, to determine.

Publishers archives, library records, letters and diaries of individuals, reading lists, authors' estimates are often used to gauge a book's sale. Its serialization and dramatization, its effect upon contemporary style, custom and language, its persistence in the folk memory must also be considered.

Yet while each of these is important none supplies a final answer.

Publishers' records are gone or unavailable. Two of the oldest houses, J. B. Lippincott and Harper & Brothers, both suffered disastrous fires in the last century. Early library records often reflect a director's or a committee's taste, not the patrons'. Diaries, letters and reading lists, too, are more apt to mention "good" books and forget the "trash."

Authors' estimates are often a kind of barometer indicating the emotional climate of the moment. If one wishes to win sympathy, forestall an appeal, escape a responsibility, sales figures drop sharply, in-

213

evitably to rise again in the presence of prospective publishers, loyal readers, dangerous rivals and inquiring reporters. Even with the best will in the world many nineteenth-century writers could not have quoted their exact sales. Titles were often sold outright, or subcontracted by the original purchaser to other houses, or simply appropriated with no notice or fee and republished with slight changes in title and text.

Lyle H. Wright, in "A Statistical Survey of American Fiction; 1774-1850" (*Huntington Library Quarterly*, II, 1938-39), suggests that the number of editions a given title achieves within a stated period reflects its popularity with some accuracy.

The size of an edition can vary widely, of course, and occasionally an author may not permit reprinting (Mrs. Southworth for reasons important to her refused many offers to reissue one of her most exciting tales, *The Hidden Hand*), but admitting these qualifying factors, Mr. Wright's method seems one of the best for determining relative popularity.

Publishers are businessmen, privy to trade secrets, both fact and gossip, on which to base their judgment. They made mistakes but in general they reprinted only what they knew had sold in the past and believed would continue to do in the future.

In addition to material noted earlier and specific references below, interviews, articles, obituaries, open letters to and from readers and writers of the domestic novel in contemporary newspapers and magazines provided useful information as did critical notices, reviews and advertisements of the novels as they appeared.

Files of *The Author, The American Bookseller, The American Publishers' Circular and Literary Gazette, Book News, The Book Trade Monthly, The Bookman, Current Literature, The Literary World, Norton's Literary Adviser* and its successors, and *Publishers' Weekly* all contained important, if brief, notes.

Abbot, Edith. *Women in Industry,* New York, 1910

Abell, Aaron I. *The Urban Impact on American Protestantism,* Cambridge, Massachusetts, 1943

Adams, James Truslow. *Provincial Society, 1690-1763,* New York, 1927

Admari, Ralph. "Ballou, the Father of the Dime Novel," *American Book Collector,* Vol. 4, p. 121, September-October, 1933

————. "Bonner and the Ledger," *American Book Collector,* Vol. 6, p. 176, May-June, 1935

————. "House of Beadle," *American Book Collector*, Vol. 4, p. 221, November, 1933

Alden, Isabella M. (Pansy). *Memories of Yesterday*, Philadelphia, 1931

Alexander, Mary. "Rise and Decline of the Three Volume Novel," *Library Association Record*, n.s., Vol. 2, p. 150, 1924

Allibone, S. A. *A Critical Dictionaay of English Literature*, Philadelphia, 3 Vols., 1870-71

Anonymous. *Life and Beauties of Fanny Fern*, New York, 1855

————. *T. S. Arthur by One Who Knows Him*, Boston, 1873

————. "Some 'Lady Novelists' and Their Work as Seen From a Public Library," *Literary World*, Vol. 13, p. 182, June 3, 1882

Appleton's Annual Cyclopedia and Register of Important Events, New York, Vol. 1-15, 1861-75; Vol. 16-35, 1876-95; Vol. 36-42, 1896-1902

Appleton's Cyclopaedia of American Biography, New York, 1887-1889

Arnett, F. S. "Fifty Years of Uncle Tom's Cabin," *Munsey's Magazine*, Vol. 27, p. 897, September, 1902

Arthur, T. S. *Autobiography in Lights and Shadows*, New York, 1861

Baker, E. A. *The Story of the English Novel*, 10 Vols., London, 1934-39

Barnett, J. H. *Divorce and the American Divorce Novel, 1858-1937*, Philadelphia, 1939

Barry, Florence. *A Century of Children's Books*, London, 1922

Bates, Ernest. *American Faith. Its Religious, Political and Economic Foundation*, New York, 1940

Beard, Charles A. and Mary R. *The Rise of American Civilization*, New York, 1927

Beard, Mary R. *Women as a Force in History*, New York, 1946

Beers, Henry. *Nathaniel Parker Willis*, Boston, 1885

Benson, Mary S. *Women in Eighteenth Century America*, New York, 1935

Birkhead, Edith. "Sentiment and Sensibility in the Eighteenth Century Novel," *Essays and Studies of the English Association*, Vol. 11, 1925

Bishop, W. H. "Story Paper Literature," *Atlantic Monthly*, Vol. 44, p. 383, September, 1879

Black, Frank G. *The Epistolary Novel in the Late Eighteenth Century*, Eugene, Oregon, 1940

Blankenship, Russell. *American Literature as an Expression of the National Mind*, New York, 1931

Bogart, Ernest L. *An Economic History of the United States*, New York, 1930

Bolton, C. K. *The Elizabeth Whitman Peabody Mystery*, Massachusetts, 1912

——. *Circulating Libraries in Boston 1765-1865*, Publication of the Colonial Society of Massachusetts, Vol. 11, p. 196, Boston, 1910

Booth, B. A. "Taste in Annuals," *American Literature*, Vol. 14, p. 299, November, 1942

Bowne, E. S. *A Girl's Life Eighty Years Ago*, New York, 1887

Boyle, Regis Louise, *Mrs. E.D.E.N. Southworth, Novelist*, Washington, 1939

Boynton, P. *Literature and American Life*, New York, 1936

Branch, E. D. *The Sentimental Years, 1836-1860*, New York, 1934

Brewton, William W. "St. Elmo and St. Twel'mo," *Saturday Review of Literature*, Vol. 5, p. 1123, June 22, 1929

Brooks, Van Wyck. *The Flowering of New England, 1815-1865*, New York, 1936

——. *New England: Indian Summer*, New York, 1940

——. *The World of Washington Irving*, Philadelphia, 1944

Brown, Herbert Ross. *The Sentimental Novel in America 1789-1860*, Durham, North Carolina, 1940

Brown, Janet. *The Saga of Elsie Dinsmore; A Study in Nineteenth Century Sensibility*, University of Buffalo Studies, Vol. 17, No. 3, Monographs in English 4, 1945

Bryce, James B. *The American Commonwealth*, 2 Vols., New York, 1920

Buchan, John. *The Novel and the Fairy Tale*, The English Association Pamphlet No. 79, July, 1931

Burnett, Frances Hodgson. *The One I Knew Best of All*, New York, 1893

Burnett, Vivian. *The Romantick Lady*, New York, 1927

Calhoun, Arthur W. *Social History of the American Family*, 3 Vols., Cleveland, 1918

Calkins, Ernest Elmo. "St. Elmo, or Named for a Best Seller," *Saturday Review of Literature*, Vol. 21, December 16, 1939

Cambridge History of American Literature, 4 Vols., New York, 1917-21

Carter, Maude. "Caroline Lee Hentz, Sentimentalist of the Fifties," Thesis, Birmingham Southern College, Birmingham, Alabama, 1937

Cherrington, Edward. *Evolution of Prohibition in the United States of America*, Westerville, Ohio, 1920

Coad, Oral Sumner. "The Gothic Element in American Literature," *Journal of English and Germanic Philology*, Vol. 24, p. 1, 1925

Cole, Arthur Charles. *The Irrepressible Conflict, 1850-1865*, New York, 1934

Compton, F. E. *Subscription Books*, fourth of R. R. Bowker Memorial Lectures, New York, 1939

Cowie, Alexander. *The Rise of the American Novel*, New York, 1948

———. "The Vogue of the Domestic Novel, 1850-1870," *South Atlantic Quarterly*, Vol. 41, October, 1942

Cruse, Amy. *The Englishman and His Books in the Early Nineteenth Century*, London, 1930.

———. *The Victorians and Their Books, 1837-1887*, London, 1935

Curti, Merle E. "Dime Novels and The American Tradition," *Yale Review*, n.s., Vol. 26, p. 761, 1937

———. *The Growth of American Thought*, New York, 1943

Dall, C. H. *The Romance of the Association, or One Last Glimpse of Charlotte Temple and Eliza Wharton*, Cambridge, 1875

Davidson, James W. *Living Writers of the South*, New York, 1869

Delafield, Mrs. E. M. *Ladies and Gentlemen in Victorian Fiction*, New York, 1937

Derby, J. C. *Fifty Years Among Authors, Books and Publishers*, New York, 1884

Deutsch, Helen. *Psychology of Women*, 2 Vols., London, 1947

Dexter, Elizabeth Anthony. *Colonial Women of Affairs*, Boston, 1924

Dictionary of American Biography, New York, 1928-36

Dodd, Mead and Company, The First Hundred Years, New York, 1939

Downing, Margaret B. "Literary Landmarks," *Records of the Colonial Historical Society*, Vol. 19, p. 22, Washington, 1916

Dunlap, George A. *The City in the American Novel 1789-1900*, Philadelphia, 1934

Dunlop, John. *History of Fiction*, Philadelphia, 1842

Dunning, A. E. *Sunday School Library*, New York, 1884

Eckert, R. P. "Friendly Fragrant Fanny Ferns," *Colophon*, Vol. 5, p. 18, September, 1934

Egan, M. F. *Confessions of a Book Lover*, New York, 1922

———. *Recollections of a Happy Life*, New York, 1924

Ellis, M. "The Author of the First American Novel," *American Literature*, Vol. 4, p. 359, 1933

Evans, Charles. *American Bibliography*, New York, 1941-42

Fehlandt, A. F. *A Century of Drink Reform in the United States,* New York, 1904

Fidler, William Perry. *Augusta Evans Wilson,* University, Alabama, 1952

————. "Augusta Evans Wilson as a Confederate Propagandist," *Alabama Review,* January, 1949

Fields, Annie. *Life and Letters of Harriet Beecher Stowe,* Cambridge, Massachusetts, 1897

Finley, Ruth E. *Lady of Godey's, Sarah Josepha Hale,* Philadelphia, 1931

Fish, Carl Russell. *The Rise of the Common Man, 1830-1850,* New York, 1950

Freeman, Julia D. *Women of the South Distinguished in Literature,* New York, 1861

Fullerton, B. M. *Selected Bibliography of American Literature, 1775-1900,* New York, 1932

Furness, Clifton. *The Genteel Female,* New York, 1931

Gaines, F. P. *The Southern Plantation,* New York, 1924

Garnsey, Caroline J. "Ladies' Magazines to 1850," *New York Public Library Bulletin,* Vol. 58, No. 2, February, 1954

Garrison, W. E. *The March of Faith,* New York, 1933

Gold, Louis. "Laura Jean Libbey," *American Mercury,* Vol. 24, p. 47, September, 1931

Goodrich, S. G. *Recollections of a Life Time,* New York, 1856

Graham, Abbie. *Ladies in Revolt,* New York, 1934

Green, Harry C. and Mary W. *Pioneer Mothers of America,* New York, 1912

Green, Evarts B. *The Revolutionary Generation, 1763-1790,* New York, 1943

Groves, Ernest R. *The American Woman,* New York, 1944

Growoll, Adolph. *Book Trade Bibliography in the United States in the XIX Century,* New York, 1898

Hacker, Helen M. "Women as a Minority Group," *Social Forces,* Vol. 30, p. 60, October, 1951

Haight, Gordon. *Mrs. Sigourney, the Sweet Singer of Hartford,* New Haven, Connecticut, 1930

Haldeman, Julius E. *The First Hundred Million,* New York, 1928

Hale, Sarah J. *Woman's Record,* New York, 3rd revised edition, 1870

Halsey, Francis Whiting. *Women Authors of Our Day in Their Homes,* New York, 1903

Harkins, E. F. *Famuos Authors,* Boston, 1901

Harland, Marion. *Marion Harland's Autobiography*, New York, Harper & Brothers, 1910

Harper, J. Henry. *The House of Harper*, New York, 1912

Hart, John Seely. *Female Prose Writers of America*, Philadelphia, revised edition, 1855

Hart, James D. *The Oxford Companion to American Literature*, New York, 1956, 3rd revised edition

————. *The Popular Book*, New York, 1950

Harvey, Charles M. "The Dime Novel in American Life," *The Atlantic Monthly*, Vol. 100, p. 37, July, 1907

Hill, Joseph A. *Women in Gainful Occupations, 1870-1920*, Census Report, Washington, 1929

Hockey, Dorothy C. "The Good and The Beautiful," unpublished doctoral dissertation, Western Reserve University, Cleveland, Ohio

Inglis, Ruth. "An Objective Approach to the Relationship Between Fiction and Sociology," *American Sociological Review*, Vol. 3, p. 527, 1936

Jackson, Joseph. *Literary Landmarks of Philadelphia*, Philadelphia, 1939

Johannsen, Albert. *The House of Beadle and Adams and Its Dime and Nickel Novels*, Norman, Oklahoma, 1950

Johnson, J. G. *Southern Fiction Prior to 1860*, Charlottesville, 1909

Jordan, Alice M. *From Rollo to Tom Sawyer*, Boston, 1948

Keep, A. B. *History of the New York Society Library*, New York, 1908

Kelly, James. *American Catalogue of Books, 1861-1871*, New York, 1938

Kirk, John F. *A Supplement to Allibone's Critical Dictionary of English Literature*, 2 Vols., Philadelphia, 1891

Klein, Viola. *The Feminine Character*, New York, 1949

Krout, John Allen, and Fox, Dixon Ryan. *The Completion of Independence*, New York, 1944

Krout, John A. *The Origins of Prohibition*, New York, 1925

Kunitz, Stanley J., and Haycroft, Howard. *American Authors, 1600-1900*, New York, 1938

————. *Authors Today and Yesterday*, New York, 1934

Laski, Marghanita. *Mrs. Ewing, Mrs. Molesworth and Mrs. Hodgson Burnett*, New York, 1951

Lawrence, Margaret. *The School of Femininity*, New York, 1936

Leavis, Q. D. *Fiction and the Reading Public*, London, 1932

Lehmann-Haupt, Hellmut. *The Book in America*, New York, 1939

Lingelbach, William E. *Approaches to American Social History*, New York, 1937

Livermore, Mary A. *My Story of the War*, Hartford, Connecticut, 1888

Loshe, Lillie D. *The Early American Novel*, New York, 1930

Lynch, Denis Tilden. *The Wild Seventies*, New York, 1941

MacCarthy, B. G. *Women Writers, Their Contribution to The English Novel, 1621-1744*, Cork, 1944

Mansfield, Edward D. *Legal Rights of Women*, Salem, Massachusetts, 1845

————. *Memoirs of the Life of Dr. Daniel Drake*, Cincinnati, 1855

Martin, Charlotte E. *The Story of Brockport for 100 Years, 1829-1929*, Brockport, 1929

McDonald, Barbara Ann. "The Philosophy of the Middle Class of the 1870's as Revealed in Popular American Fiction," Unpublished thesis, Columbia University, New York

McDowell, T. "Last Words of a Sentimental Heroine," *American Literature*, Vol. 4, p. 174, 1932

McDowell, Tremaine. "Sensibility in the Eighteenth Century American Novel," *Studies in Philology*, Vol. 24, p. 383, July, 1927

Mill, John S. *The Subjection of Women*, New York, 1874

Miller, William. *The Book Industry*, New York, 1949

Minniegerode, Meade. *The Fabulous Forties*, New York, 1924

Mitchell, Donald G. *American Lands and Letters*, New York, 1897-99

Mott, Frank Luther. *Golden Multitudes*, New York, 1947

————. *History of the American Magazine*, 3 Vols., Cambridge, Massachusetts, 1938

Mumford, Lewis. *The Brown Decades*, New York, 1931

National Cyclopedia of American Biography, 39 Vols., New York, 1893-1954

Neff, Wanda. *Victorian Working Women*, New York, 1929

Nevins, Allan. *The Emergence of Modern America, 1865-78*, New York, 1927

Noel, Mary. *Villains Galore*, New York, 1954

Oberholtzer, Ellis P. *A Literary History of Philadelphia*, Philadelphia, 1906

O'Connell, J. J. "When Second Hand Books were Best Sellers," *American Book Collector*, Vol. 2, p. 138, August-September, 1932

Olmstead, Mrs. M. H. "Caroline Lee Hentz," *Beadle's Monthly*, Vol. 1, p. 520, 1866

Orgain, Kate. *Southern Authors in Poetry and Prose*, New York, 1908

Page, Thomas Nelson. *The Old South*, New York, 1925

Parrington, Vernon L. *Main Currents in American Thought*, New York, 1948

Parton, James. *Fanny Fern, A Memorial Volume*, New York, 1872

Pattee, F. L. *The Feminine Fifties*, New York, 1940

———. *The First Century of American Literature, 1770-1870* New York, 1935

Pearson, Edmund. *Dime Novels*, Boston, 1929

Pickett, LaSalle. *Literary Hearthstones of Dixie*, Philadelphia, 1912

Pierson, Ralph. "A Few Literary Highlights of 1851-52," *American Book Collector*, Vol. 2, p. 156, August-September, 1932

———. "Some Reading Material of the 1880s," *American Book Collector*, Vol. 2, p. 205, October, 1932

Porter, Kirk H. *A History of Suffrage in the United States*, Chicago, 1918

Putnam, Emily. *The Lady*, New York, 1933

Putnam, George Haven. *A Memoir of George Palmer Putnam*. New York, 1903

Quinn, Arthur H. *American Fiction*, New York, 1936

———. *A History of the American Drama from the Beginning to the Civil War*, New York, 1923

Raddin, George G., Jr. *An Early New York Library of Fiction*, New York, 1940

Raverat, Gwen. *Period Piece*, New York, 1952

Redden, Sister Mary M. *The Gothic Fiction in the American Magazines, 1765-1800*, Washington, 1939

Reppelier, Agnes. "Little Pharisees of Fiction," *Scribners*, Vol. 20, p. 718, 1896

Robbins, J. A. *Fees Paid to Certain Authors Between 1840-50*, Charlottesville, Virginia, 1949-50

Roorbach, O. A. *Bibliotheca Americana, 1820-61*, London, 1861

Rowell, George P. *Forty Years an Advertising Agent*, New York, 1902

Rusk, R. L. *The Literature of the Middle Western Frontier*, 2 Vols., New York, 1925 and 1926

Rutherford, Mildred. *American Authors*, Atlanta, Georgia, 1894

———. *The South in Historical Literature*, Atlanta, Georgia, 1907

Sabin, Joseph. *A Dictionary of Books Relating to America*, 29 Vols., New York, 1868-1936

St. Louis *Post Dispatch*. "They Dip Their Pens in Gore," August 12, 1888

Schlesinger, A. M. *Learning How to Behave*, New York, 1946

———. *The Rise of the City, 1878-98*, New York, 1933

Shove, Raymond Howard. *Cheap Book Production in the United States, 1870-1891*, Urbana, Illinois, 1937

Shurter, R. L. "Mrs. Hannah Webster Foster and the Early American Novel," American Literature, Vol. 4, p. 306, 1932

Spiller, Robert E.; Johnson, T. H.; Thorp, Willard; Canby, H. S. *Literary History of the United States*, 3 Vols., 1948

Sprague, John F. *New York, the Metropolis*, New York, 1893

Spruill, Julia Cherry. *Women's Life and Work in the Southern Colonies*, Chapel Hill, North Carolina, 1938

Stearns, Bertha M. "Before Godey's," *American Literature*, Vol. 10, p. 248, 1939

———. "Early New England Magazines for Ladies," *New England Quarterly*, Vol. 2, June 3, 1929

Stern, Madeline. "Louisa M. Alcott, an Appraisal," *New England Quarterly*, Vol. 22, p. 475, December, 1949

Stevens, George. *Best Sellers*, London, 1939

Stokes, Olivia E. P. *Letters and Memories of Susan and Anna Warner*. New York, 1925

Stowe, C. E. *Harriet Beecher Stowe*, Boston, 1911

Stuart, Arabella W. *The Lives of the Three Mrs. Judsons*, Auburn, New York, 1853

Sweet, W. W. *Religion in the Development of American Culture*, New York, 1952

———. *Revivalism in America*, New York, 1944

———. *The Story of Religions in America*, New York, 1930

Tandy, Jeannette. "Pro-Slavery Propaganda in American Fiction of the Fifties," *Southern Atlantic Quarterly*, Vol. 21, p. 65, 1922

Tarbell, Ida M. *The Nationalizing of Business, 1878-1898*, New York, 1936

Taylor, John T. *Early Opposition to the Novel*, New York, 1943

Taylor, Walter F. *The Economic Novel in America*, Chapel Hill, North Carolina, 1942

Terhune, Albert Payson. *To the Best of My Memory*, New York, 1930

Thompson, R. *American Annuals and Literary Gift Books, 1825-1865*, New York, 1936

Trubner, Nathan. *Trubner's Bibliographical Guide to American Literature*, London, 1859

Truxal, Andrew, and Merrill, Francis. *The Family in American Life*. New York, 1947

Tryon, Walter, and Charvat, William. *Cost Books of Ticknor and Fields*, Bibliographical Society of America, 1949

Turner, Frederick J. *The Frontier in American History*, New York, 1921

Turner, L. D. *Anti-Slavery Sentiment in American Literature Prior to 1865*, Washington, D. C., 1929

Vail, R. W. G. *Susanna Haswell Rowson, the Author of Charlotte Temple*, Worcester, 1933

Van Doren, Carl. *The American Novel*, New York, 1940

Vedder, Henry. *American Writers Today*, New York, 1910

Violette, Augusta G. *Economic Feminism in American Literature Prior to 1848*, University of Maine Studies, Series 2, No. 2, Orono, Maine, 1925

Walter, Frank K. "A Poor But Respectable Relation—The Sunday School Library," *Library Quarterly*, Vol. 12, p. 371, 1942

Warner, Anna B. *Susan Warner*, New York, 1904

Wecter, Dixon. *The Saga of American Society: A Record of Social Aspiration, 1607-1937*, New York, 1937

Wegelin, Oscar. *Early American Fiction*, New York, 1929

Whichard, Lindsay. "C. L. Hentz, Pro-Slavery Propagandist," M.A. thesis, Chapel Hill, North Carolina, 1951

Willard, Frances, and Livermore, Mary. *American Women*, revised edition, Chicago, 1901

Williams, Stanley T. *The American Spirit in Letters*, New Haven, 1926

Wilson, Edmund. *The Wound and the Bow*, Boston, 1941

Wilson, Forrest. *Crusader in Crinoline*, Philadelphia, 1941

Wolfe, Theodore. *Literary Haunts and Homes*, Philadelphia, 1899

Woody, T. *A History of Women's Education in the United States*, Lancaster, Pennsylvania, 1929

Wright, Lyle H. *American Fiction, 1774-1850: A Contribution Toward a Bibliography*, San Marino, California, 1939

———. "Propaganda in Early American Fiction," *Bibliographical Society of American Papers*, Vol. 33, p. 98

———. "A Statistical Survey of American Fiction 1774-1850," *Huntington Library Quarterly*, Vol. 2, p. 309, 1938-1939

Wright, Walter F. *Sensibility in English Prose Fiction, 1760-1818*, Urbana, Illinois, 1937

Wynn, William T. *Southern Literature*, New York, 1932

INDEX

Index

Index

Index

Set in Linotype Fairfield
Format by Robert Cheney
Manufactured by The Haddon Craftsmen, Inc.
Published by HARPER & BROTHERS, *New York*